I0799201

MONSTER HUNTING
HUNTING
WEREWOLVES
GRAEME DAVIS
ROSEN PUBLISHING
New York

This edition published in 2017 by

The Rosen Publishing Group, Inc.
29 East 21st Street
New York, NY 10010

Additional end matter copyright © 2017 by The Rosen Publishing Group, Inc.

All rights reserved. No part of this book may be reproduced in any form without permission in writing from the publisher, except by a reviewer.

Library of Congress Cataloging-in-Publication Data

Names: Davis, Graeme, author.
Title: Hunting werewolves / Graeme Davis.
Description: New York : Rosen Publishing, [2017] | Series: Monster hunting
Identifiers: LCCN 2016035771 | ISBN 9781499465341 (library bound)
Subjects: LCSH: Werewolves.
Classification: LCC GR830.W4 D38 2017 | DDC 398.24/54—dc23
LC record available at https://lccn.loc.gov/2016035771

Manufactured in the United States of America

© Osprey Publishing, 2015
All rights reserved
This edition published by Rosen Publishing by arrangement with Osprey Publishing, an imprint of Bloomsbury Publishing Plc.

Contents

Introduction

A few years ago, I received an email from Joseph McCullough, the author of *Zombies: A Hunter's Guide*. During the course of writing his book, Joe had been granted unprecedented access to the US Army's 34th Specialist Regiment, nicknamed the Nightmen, and had been approached to compile an official unit history of this remarkable group of men and women. Impressed by what he had seen of my research into the Knights Templar, Joe invited me to collaborate with him on the Nightmen project. Both flattered and intrigued, I agreed and began working on background research.

It was while I was researching the 34th's operations in World War II – in particular, their encounters with the *Werwolf* guerillas of SS Obergruppenführer Hans-Adolf Prützmann in Cologne and elsewhere – that I first heard of the Tyana Institute. I began with orthodox sources, and made a number of inquiries through contacts in various European universities, but this initial research hit a dead end.

In the interests of the Nightmen project, I should probably have moved on. However, the few snippets of information I had unearthed on the Tyana Institute convinced me that there was more to find. I turned to less orthodox avenues of inquiry, and what I found fully bore out my first instincts. There was a story here, I knew – though what I could not have anticipated was just how many stories there were, and how many different groups were involved. I called Joe, and after looking at my initial findings he agreed to give me time to continue this line of research.

Werewolves are far from unknown. From the Big Bad Wolf of nursery tales to the computer-generated beasts of the movies, they have earned a prominent place in popular culture. Everyone knows that one bite from a werewolf is enough to pass the curse of lycanthropy on to the victim; that the full moon forces them to change shape and surrender their human reason to savage animal passions; that wolfsbane and silver are their only weaknesses. Almost no one knows that there are many forms of lycanthropy, and not all of them are occult in nature.

The following pages tell a few of the stories I have uncovered. There is much work still to be done, many facts to be verified and many more leads and sidetracks to be followed. A definitive treatment of the subject may take a lifetime – perhaps more than one lifetime – and the deeper one delves, the more elusive hard information becomes.

I still hope, one day, to return to the history of the Nightmen. Of course, there is always the chance that when I do, I will stumble upon yet another irresistible side-track. Until then, I offer my thanks to Joe for the email that began this whole journey, to the personnel of the 34th who were unfailingly patient and helpful in answering my questions, and to others – many others – who for various reasons prefer to remain anonymous.

The 17th-century painting *Jupiter and Lycaon* by Jan Cossiers. In the ancient Greek myth, Lycaon decided to test the god Zeus (called Jupiter by the Romans) by serving him human flesh. Zeus punished Lycaon by turning him into a wolf. Many believe that Lycaon was the father of all werewolves and that the original virus can be traced back to him. Others think he is just one more example of a man cursed by dark sorcery.

Chapter 1 – Viral Werewolves

The viral werewolf is sometimes called the "true" or "classic" werewolf. This is the werewolf of movies and literature: active around the full moon; vulnerable to silver; capable of transforming into beast or "wolf man" form; and able to pass on its condition through a bite or scratch. While viral werewolves are not the only werewolves, they are by far the best-known type.

Based on reports dating back to Classical antiquity, scientists believe that viral werewolves originated somewhere in southeastern Europe, in the heavily wooded, mountainous country now occupied by Romania, Hungary, Slovakia, and eastern Austria, and stretching southward into the Balkans, Bulgaria, Macedonia, and northern Greece.

In ancient times this form of lycanthropy was mostly confined within the borders of that region, known then as Moesia and Dacia, owing to its remoteness and the lack of significant outside trade. The region's evil reputation as a haunt of werewolves, vampires, witches, and other monsters also contributed to its isolation.

The area lay largely outside the bounds of the Roman and Byzantine empires, so Classical writers like Pausanias and Pliny the Elder record only occasional rumors of lycanthropy in the area. They make no distinction between these viral lycanthropes and the werewolf cults of southern Greece and Anatolia; to them, all werewolves were alike. However, a few documents from the Roman provinces of Moesia and Dacia contain hints of the truth.

Crassus the Younger, the grandson of Octavian's colleague-turned-rival, conquered Moesia for Rome in 29–27 BC, subduing an area that covers present-day Serbia, Macedonia, and adjoining parts of Romania and Bulgaria. However, the emperor Augustus denied him the usual honors and titles due to the conqueror of a new province, and it was only after some persuasion that he was even permitted a triumphal procession on his return to Rome. It was rumored that he had become unpredictable following a wound received on the battlefield; the poet Catullus, ever a thorn in the emperor's side, published a scurrilous verse that had Crassus urinating on his own doorpost and sniffing the backsides of every woman he met. Crude as these images are, they strongly suggest that Crassus had contracted lycanthropy in Moesia. Also interesting is the fact that he produced no natural heirs, adopting the son of the old but declining Piso family.

While most werewolves spend a majority of their time in either human or wolf form, it is the rarer wolf man form that has caught the popular imagination thanks to modern media. Illustration by Hauke Kock.

It was more than a century before the Roman Empire regarded Moesia as stable. In AD 87, the emperor Trajan used it as a springboard for his Dacian campaign, which is recorded on Trajan's Column in Rome. The Dacian Wars dragged on for almost 20 years, and Dacia remained a battleground until it was finally abandoned in AD 275.

Roman exploitation brought Roman administrators, Roman tax-collectors, and Roman merchants into the area, creating more vectors for the spread of lycanthropy across Europe, North Africa, and the Middle East. In AD 193, the emperor Pertinax used the Praetorian Guard to suppress a cult of Selene Sanguinea ("the Blood Moon") which had arisen in Rome, citing "the great violence of its rites and its profaning of the Lupercalia" (a very ancient Roman festival honoring the she-wolf who had suckled Romulus and Remus). His enemies claimed the move was political, since his predecessor, the notorious

Commodus, had been an initiate of the cult, but documents in the Vatican's secret archives record a full-blown outbreak of lycanthropy in Rome between AD 190 and 192. Pertinax was murdered shortly after ordering the suppression of the Blood Moon cult, apparently by Praetorians who were secretly members – and very possibly lycanthropes – themselves.

After the fall of Rome, Moesia and Dacia were occupied by the expanding Goths and Huns. Some writers believe that it was through the Goths – originally from the region of Götland in modern Sweden – that lycanthropy reached Scandinavia and gave rise to the famous berserkers and *ulfhednar* of the Viking Age. The Goths were followed by a succession of short-lived states until the Ottoman Empire conquered the area in the 14th century, setting the stage for an eastward spread of lycanthropy.

In 1542, the area around Constantinople (modern Istanbul) was so overrun with werewolves that the Ottoman emperor Suleiman the Magnificent was forced to take action. In one hunt alone, according to contemporary writers, Suleiman and his janissaries killed 150 of the creatures who were "prowling the streets and lanes of the city."

By now, lycanthropy was well established across Europe and the Middle East, and with the dawning of the Age of Exploration its worldwide spread became inevitable. As early as 1693, a settlement on Cape Ann in the Massachusetts colony had gained the local name "Dogtown" along with a reputation as a haunt of witches and shapeshifters. Since then, werewolves have been reported across North America as well as in their older European haunts.

Case Studies

Châlus, 12th century

The 12th-century English writer Gervase of Tilbury tells of one Calcevayra, who was active around the town of Châlus in western France. At the full moon this individual "was wont to go apart to a distant spot and there stripping himself mother-naked… he rolled to and fro in the sand until he rose up in the form of a wolf, raging with a wolf's fierce appetites. With gaping jaws and lolling tongue he rushed violently upon his prey." Unfortunately Gervase neglected to record how this Calcevayra first became a werewolf, or what became of him when his nature was discovered.

OPPOSITE:
In the 12th through 16th centuries, werewolf incidents were especially common in France and Germany. These werewolves preyed on livestock, children, and occasionally lone women. Some lycanthropes lived undetected for decades and confessed to scores of killings at their trials.

Werewolf detection was in its infancy at this time. Most arrests depended upon the reports of neighbors, which could be unreliable. The surest proof was when a local person showed identical wounds to those inflicted on an attacking wolf.

Wyoming, 1906

Celebrity encounters with werewolves are very rare indeed, but in 1906 William F. Cody, the showman known the world over as Buffalo Bill, had a desperate encounter with a creature that he described as a werewolf.

The story has been dismissed by some scholars as another piece of the self-promoting fiction with which Cody habitually surrounded himself, and the body of the supposed werewolf was never recovered. However, the archives of

A posed photo of the famous 'Wyoming Werewolf Posse' that supposedly killed or captured half a dozen werewolves in the 1880s. (Library of Congress)

the Tyana Institute contain a letter to Senator (and former Wyoming governor) Francis E. Warren from respected Wyoming academic Grace Raymond Hebard in which she states that "I have personally interviewed several people from Wolf River Canyon and the surrounding area (transcripts enclosed) and see no reason to suppose that Cody's tale is false." Frustratingly, the transcripts referred to in the letter seem to have gone missing.

Wolf River Canyon takes its name from an Arapahoe tradition, and despite some evidence to the contrary, it seems possible that the creature Cody encountered may have been a skinwalker rather than a werewolf of the European type. The Tyana Institute sent an expedition to the area in 1908 under cover of a survey for the Shoshone Dam project, but it failed to trace any local traditions of either werewolves or skinwalkers, and its report was inconclusive.

Creation

As its name suggests, viral lycanthropy is spread by contact. The most common form of transmission is through a bite or scratch that does not prove fatal. A person who survives a werewolf's attack is doomed to become a werewolf in turn, changing shape uncontrollably as soon as the next full moon rises. Unless the new werewolf is contained he or she will run amok, maddened by new and unfamiliar animal passions, and cause untold carnage.

Since the birth of germ theory in the 18th century, researchers have looked for some micro-organism – a parasite, bacterium, or virus – that causes lycanthropy. Research over the last two centuries has established that lycanthropy is a separate condition from rabies, porphyria, and various other afflictions that have been suggested as a scientific explanation for the condition. However, the virus itself has not yet been identified.

A determined and well-funded – if secret – search for the lycanthropy virus has been under way since the 1930s, but has yet to yield any definitive results. Current research is focused on two distinct avenues: a virus that cannot be

A 16th-century depiction of a werewolf. One of the major difficulties of werewolf studies is the paucity of information regarding most historical occurrences. This 16th-century drawing offers no visual clues about the type of werewolf, although given the time and place (Germany) either a viral or cursed werewolf seems most likely. (Mary Evans)

detected with existing equipment, perhaps because it is an isomer of another well-known virus whose structural peculiarities give it unexpected properties; and a currently known virus that interacts with the DNA of susceptible victims to cause lycanthropy in them alone, while leaving others unaffected.

Several reports dating back to the Middle Ages suggest that viral lycanthropy can also be inherited from one or both parents. Lycanthropy was common among the post-medieval aristocracy of Courland in modern Latvia and Lithuania, for example, and the inherited susceptibility, or perhaps the virus itself, may have been passed down in increasing concentrations through the restricted aristocratic gene pool. However, it is not inevitable that the child of a werewolf will also be a werewolf. For example Ulf Bjalfason, the grandfather of the Icelandic hero Egill Skallagrímsson, was a known werewolf called Kveldulf ("evening wolf") by his neighbors. However, neither Ulf's son Skallagrimm nor his grandson Egill ever showed any signs of lycanthropy.

Documents from the Tyana Institute note the Sicilian belief that a child conceived at the new moon will become a werewolf. However, Benjamin Franklin discounts it as superstition in a letter to Thomas Jefferson:

> The New Moon occurring thirteen times in each year, which is one night out of each twenty-eight, and at all times of the year so that the effect of any particular season may be discounted, inclines me to regard such arguments as invalid; for surely, if it were true, then lycanthropy must surely manifest in one man or woman of each twenty-eight, and yet these creatures are rarely reported even in our greatest and most populous cities. If there be any lunar influence at work, I confess myself more inclined to believe that one upon whose face the rays of the moon fall upon a certain Wednesday or Friday in summer may be afflicted with

VAMPIRES AND WEREWOLVES

In modern horror literature and film, vampires and werewolves have become traditional enemies, but this was not always the case. The folklore of Greece makes very little distinction between them, often using the same word, *vrykolaka*, to describe both creatures. Sabine Baring-Gould cites a Greek superstition that a dead werewolf is doomed to rise from the grave as a vampire.

Bram Stoker may have referenced this belief, consciously or otherwise. His Count Dracula is seen to have an affinity for wolves, and in the short story *Dracula's Guest* – an out-take from the original manuscript that was published posthumously by Stoker's widow – the protagonist's life is saved by a gigantic and possibly supernatural wolf, apparently at Dracula's behest.

Over the past 300 years, though, studies of both vampires and werewolves have failed to find any evidence of significant physiological or supernatural links between the two.

this condition; such a thing has often been said to cause the mania we call *lunacy,* tho' I never heard of any trial or experiment that bore out either proposition.

Identification and Threat

According to folklore, viral werewolves show two main signs of their condition while in human form; however, these have been found to be unreliable as means of field identification.

The first is that the eyebrows meet, forming what is commonly called a "unibrow." This characteristic is by no means restricted to lycanthropes, however, and has become part of a common Western stereotype image of eastern Europeans. In addition, it is easily disguised by shaving, plucking, or waxing.

The second is the unusual length of the ring finger, which is longer than the middle finger in some individuals. While it is a more reliable indicator than the eyebrows, it is difficult to observe in an unwilling subject, and it is by no means universal.

Other traditional signs, such as hair on the palms, casting a wolf's shadow, and leaving wolf tracks instead of footprints, have been found to be pure invention.

The most obvious identifying characteristic of a viral werewolf is its ability to assume the transitional "wolf man" form in addition to purely human and lupine forms. Newly infected viral werewolves often adopt this form spontaneously as the human and wolf sides of their nature struggle for dominance, but more experienced shapeshifters can assume wolf man form at will.

In wolf form, it has been claimed that the eyes of a werewolf remain human in appearance. Again, this is difficult to observe under field conditions, where distance, poor light, and the subject's motion do not generally permit such close observation. The main visible difference between a human eye and the eye of a normal wolf is in the amount of white that shows, and it is not uncommon for the whites of the eyes to be visible in angry or fearful canines.

A typical Hollywood depiction of a werewolf. Although the look is basically accurate, Hollywood has done more than anything to sow confusion and spread misinformation about werewolves. (Photos 12 / Alamy)

Many field biologists have remarked on the gaze of a wild wolf, saying that it conveys the impression of an almost human-like intelligence but admitting that this is a very subjective matter with no scientific basis. So far it has been impossible to draw any conclusions about werewolf eyes by autopsy or examination of tranquilized werewolves, because death or unconsciousness invariably trigger a return to human form.

While in wolf form, viral werewolves retain their human intelligence but gain the wolf's advantages of strength, speed, ferocity, as well as superior hearing, smell and low-light vision. Old Norse sources claim that a shapeshifter's strength was greater than that of either man or wolf; the wolf's strength was added to the man's rather than merely replacing it.

Although they may retain human intelligence, shifted werewolves – especially inexperienced ones – do not necessarily retain human control. Animal instincts are strong, and both practice and willpower are required if the werewolf is to overcome them. Those who fail to do so fall into what Old Norse writers called the *gandreid* or wolf-ride, driven by what Sabine Baring-Gould calls "the rage and malignity of the creatures [sic] whose powers and passions he has assumed."

The process of transforming from human to wolf form takes several minutes and is more dramatic and painful in viral werewolves than in any other kind. The werewolf is fully conscious as bones, teeth, muscles, and other tissues rearrange themselves and hair grows all over the body. An experienced werewolf can transform in a shorter time and resist the effects of shock and panic, but the experience is never a comfortable one.

Viral werewolves are at their most dangerous shortly after contracting lycanthropy. Inexperienced werewolves are easily overwhelmed by their condition and are less able to control either their transformation or their animal drives while they are transformed. They tend to rampage in a panicked state, attacking livestock and humans in an orgy of violence. Unless it is stopped quickly, a newly infected viral werewolf can cause considerable destruction and loss of life. What is worse, though, is that an inexperienced werewolf is an inefficient killer, with more chance of leaving wounded victims behind who will become werewolves in their turn and create a full-blown outbreak.

The majority of viral werewolves are detected and destroyed early in their careers. A few may survive through luck and cunning until they can master their condition and become more efficient shapeshifters and hunters – and, paradoxically, less of a threat to their human neighbors. More experienced werewolves usually take care to avoid detection, hunting in remote areas where their kills are less likely to be found. Many adopt a nomadic lifestyle, keeping on the move to avoid leaving an identifiable pattern of activity in a specific area. Some set out on a quest to understand their condition and seek a cure.

There are circumstances in which a viral werewolf is infected deliberately and given post-infection care and training to manage the condition. A new member may be inducted into an established pack, for example; an experienced werewolf may deliberately infect a chosen mate; and, of course, several governments and corporations have been known to conduct werewolf programs for military purposes. These instances are examined later in this book.

Elimination and Prevention

At the time of writing, the virus responsible for viral lycanthropy has not been identified, making it impossible to develop the necessary antigens and antivirals to prevent and treat the disease. Quarantine and extermination remain the only means of prevention. Although lycanthropy research is classified top secret by a number of countries, there are government and military quarantine and research facilities in various countries that are known or suspected to be involved in the effort to isolate the virus and develop treatments and immunization protocols.

Extract of wolfsbane, also known as aconite or monkshood, is frequently mentioned in folklore as being deadly to werewolves, perhaps because in the Middle Ages wolfsbane-tainted meat was used to control wolf populations. While wolfsbane is certainly effective in killing werewolves, it is just as dangerous to humans and other species, and there is no scientific evidence that it is especially deadly to lycanthropes.

There is a great deal more evidence in favor of the other traditional anti-werewolf weapon, silver. All viral lycanthropes exhibit a violent allergic reaction to silver, both in wolf and human form. Skin contact causes redness and irritation almost immediately, which develops into hives and blistering on prolonged contact. Wounding with silver weapons or ammunition often results in severe anaphylactic shock, which is usually fatal.

The hunt for a viral werewolf has many aspects in common with a law enforcement manhunt. Ideally it is preceded by an evidence-gathering phase in which suspects are identified and eliminated, although there is not always time when livestock and locals are in danger. Kill sites are examined by experienced trackers, who work with local experts to narrow down the range of possible lairs, and each one is swept by kill or capture teams according to the mission protocol.

Because of the high risk of infection, personnel hunting viral werewolves are routinely equipped with body armor that covers as much of the body as possible. SWAT-style combat gear is standard, and is usually augmented with additional neck protection. While discussing anti-werewolf gear with personnel from the 34th Specialist Regiment, I was told more than once that it was they (or rather, their predecessors in the Tyana Rangers) who were the original "leathernecks," and not the United States Marine Corps. Nightmen lore has it that Benjamin Franklin designed a stiff leather collar specifically for anti-werewolf and anti-vampire operations during the Revolutionary War, and the Marines copied the design to protect their necks from Corsair scimitars on "the shores of Tripoli" 25 years later during the Barbary Wars.

Some have claimed that stories of Bigfoot or the Yeti are derived from people seeing a werewolf in wolf man form; however, there is ample evidence for the independent existence of those creatures. Artwork by Hauke Kock.

When civilians are drafted in to help deal with larger outbreaks, it is sometimes necessary to improvise body armor. Football and hockey gear is often used, along with welding gloves and visored motorcycle helmets.

For kill missions, the 34th uses the M4 carbine, fitted with the 12-gauge M26 Modular Accessory Shotgun System (MASS). Carbine rounds are silver-coated if the target has been positively identified as a viral lycanthrope. The shotgun is routinely loaded with silver 00 buckshot in case the target is a viral lycanthrope wrongly identified as another type. Each squad is also equipped with a 12-gauge Pancor Jackhammer automatic shotgun, capable of firing 00 buckshot rounds at 240rpm.

THE FULL MOON

Most viral lycanthropes are very sensitive to the phases of the moon, becoming agitated and sometimes violent during the three days around the full moon. Inexperienced viral werewolves often shift uncontrollably into wolf form at this time, although the transformation can be controlled with experience and practice.

Given adequate support, a viral werewolf can learn to control his or her condition quite rapidly. According to an *Ahnenerbe* report recovered in 1945 by Operation *Paperclip* and preserved in the archives of the Imperial War Museum, "All recruits initially showed signs of agitation over the three nights of the full moon, which were especially pronounced in the newest. This was overcome through psychological conditioning, and within three months almost all were able to maintain self-control at all times and affect their transformations at will and in a controlled manner."

Capture teams are additionally equipped with the M26 Taser and incapacitating rock salt rounds in place of silver 00 buckshot. However, it is common for at least one squad member (called "Plan B" by squad-mates) to carry silver ammunition as a fail-safe. Another squad member (sometimes called "Plan A") carries either an XM42 four-barreled net launcher or a carbine-length modification of the Barrett XM500 sniper rifle firing 50-caliber tranquilizer darts, known informally as the "Squad Close-Range Incapacitating Weapon" (SCRIW).

Contrary to much werewolf lore, transformed werewolves are not completely immune to mundane weapons, although it is true that they can shrug off non-lethal wounds that would disable a human being. However, a maiming or mortal wound will normally force them to return to human form. Countless reports tell of a werewolf being discovered in human form, bearing identical wounds to those inflicted on a marauding wolf by hunters or soldiers.

Some werewolves return to human form immediately, while others run off but are found in human form shortly afterward. In a report from the *Ahnenerbe*, Nazi Germany's institute created to research the history of the Aryan race, recovered by Operation *Surgeon*, SS doctor Friedrich Weiss claims that less experienced werewolves are more prone to change spontaneously from the shock of a serious wound, while willpower and adrenaline permit more seasoned individuals to delay transformation for a short while.

Chapter 2 - Shamanic Werewolves

In this form of lycanthropy, the werewolf's body does not undergo a physical change into the form of a wolf. Instead, the human spirit leaves the human body through a process similar to astral projection, and occupies the body of a wolf. The human consciousness blends with that of the wolf, and the human body is left behind in what appears to be a deep sleep or coma. When the spirit returns to its human body, the werewolf awakens with memories of the wolf's activities.

Although this form of lycanthropy is most often associated with shamanism, it can also occur accidentally in individuals with a latent talent for astral projection. Talented but untrained individuals can experience spontaneous projection into an animal body, and most often they find themselves – whatever guilt they may feel upon waking – powerless witnesses to the animal's hunting and other activities.

The amount of control that a projected human mind can exert over its lupine host varies. Untrained shamanic werewolves are usually confused and frightened by their experience, and either cannot control the wolf-body or do not attempt to do so. They awake with feelings of guilt and shame, especially if they have witnessed the wolf making a human kill, and some are driven by this guilt to confess their supposed crime or to seek spiritual advice from their local priest. A significant proportion of the medieval werewolf trials seem to have resulted from this kind of experience.

Werewolves who are trained shamans, or are naturally strong-willed, may be able to gain control over the wolf-body. In Finland, Siberia, and other parts of the world where a strong shamanic tradition survives, it is not uncommon to encounter reports of shamanic possession of animals. Wolves are not the only species involved: experienced shamans have been known to take over the bodies of falcons, whales, deer, and other species according to their needs and the animal's abilities.

The only existent photograph of Lean Wolf, arguably the most famous and respected of all North American shamans (Library of Congress)

Most true shamans (as distinct from witches, warlocks, and wolf cultists) are members of isolated ethnic and cultural groups. In most parts of the world, shamanism has long been extinct, replaced by the polytheistic religions of the Neolithic, Bronze, and Iron ages and then by the largely monotheistic religions of the last two thousand years. However, there are a few places where unbroken traditions of shamanic-animist beliefs and practices can still be found. These include Finland and Lapland, Siberia, the Japanese island of Hokkaido, and certain remote islands off the coasts of Scotland and Ireland.

Perhaps the most significant survival of shamanic animism, though, is in the Americas. Over the last 50 years, growing interest in traditional native practices and the development of New Age and neo-pagan beliefs has led to a revival of shamanism. This has not always been welcomed by traditional practitioners, many of whom regard the predominantly Anglo newcomers as immature and without the necessary discipline to master the old ways.

According to one Native American shaman who was interviewed for this book:

> Some of these new people, they think they're going to some summer camp where they'll learn to do some kind of comic-book stuff and then they get to go home and be powerful. Their people aren't from here; they have no ties to the land and the spirits here, and they're not planning to stay here; that all makes it harder. They always want it to be easy, so they get frustrated. I show them enough to make them feel good, but not so much they become dangerous to themselves or to others. There are some folks that aren't as careful as I am, though. They like money too much, and they'll sell everything they know. That's how people wind up with power they can't handle.

Case Studies

Calmar, Sweden, 1790

In the last year of the Russo-Swedish War (1788–90), the southern Swedish province of Calmar was overrun by an unusual number of wolves. It was believed that at least some of these creatures were werewolves created by the Russians from Swedish prisoners and sent home to destabilize the area. Shortly afterward, a demoralized Sweden sued for peace on the pretext that the war was becoming prohibitively expensive.

Letters recently discovered in the archives of St. Petersburg's Hermitage Museum shed new light on the Calmar outbreak. Count Georg Magnus Sprengtporten, a pro-Russian nobleman born in Swedish-controlled Finland, writes to Catherine the Great offering to recruit "from among my countrymen an irregular force of a type never before seen outside Finland, capable of movement behind enemy lines and able to destroy Swedish morale completely, against which the enemy has no possible defense."

Native Americans hunting Buffalo while wearing wolf skins. Shamanic werewolves would also join in such hunts to help drive and confuse prey. (North Wind Picture Archives / Alamy)

Ever since Viking times, Finland has been notorious as a nation of witches and shapeshifters, and it always chafed under Swedish rule. Pending further detailed analysis of documents from the Russo-Swedish War, it seems likely that the wolves of Calmar were controlled by Finnish shamans whom Sprengtporten recruited to fight the hated Swedes. The tale of them being transformed Swedish prisoners seems to be no more than a rumor, perhaps spread deliberately to further reduce Swedish morale.

Moose Lake, Minnesota, 2012

In July of 2012, a group of biologists from the University of Minnesota traveled to the Kabetogama State Forest in the northern part of the state to conduct a field study of the local wolf population. The expedition, planned to last for three months, was abandoned after two weeks when doctoral candidate Kyle Stegman was medevaced to the Rainy Lake Medical Center in International Falls after being severely mauled by a wolf that broke into his tent.

A few weeks later, fellow student Jason Mackey sought counseling at the University's Student Health Center, complaining of nightmares and a deep sense of guilt toward Stegman, who was Mackey's rival for the affections of another student named Jennifer Ullman. After several sessions of counseling and hypnotherapy, it emerged that on the night Stegman was attacked, Mackey experienced a vivid dream in which he took the form of a wolf and attacked his rival savagely.

Mackey took an extended leave of absence, most of which he spent at the nearby Bois Forte Reservation of the Chippewa Nation. It was found that he

ASTRAL BODIES

The 19th-century French mystic Eliphas Levi speculated that a wolf was not strictly necessary for the process of shamanic lycanthropy. Instead, he suggested that an astral traveler could equally well appear to the waking eye in the form of a wolf as in his or her natural human form. Montague Summers sums up Levi's argument thus: "in the case of a man whose instinct is savage and sanguinary, his phantom will wander abroad in lupine form, whilst he sleeps painfully at home, dreaming he is a veritable wolf." Levi was anxious to explain lycanthropy in terms of his theories of astral projection, while Summers wanted to prove the official line of the Catholic Church, that it cannot exist except as a product of madness or diabolical illusion: readers can judge for themselves how well either one succeeded.

had inadvertently dreamed himself into the body of a wolf from the western Moose Lake pack, and had acted out his romantic frustrations in this form. He learned to control his dreams with the help of a Chippewa shaman, and has reported no further incidents.

CREATION

Shamanic lycanthropy normally requires a significant amount of training. As an apprentice, the shaman must first learn to master astral projection and travel before learning to cast his or her consciousness into another body, a process sometimes informally known as "skin-riding." The final step in the process is learning to suppress the host animal's will and control its body.

Exact methods vary from one shamanic tradition to another. Often the process involves a deep meditation, and in some places this is augmented by narcotic or psychedelic preparations made from local plants. Similar drugs feature in many reports of sorcerous and obsessive werewolves (which are covered in later chapters), but shamanic werewolves are distinct in their style of training and method of possession.

A shaman may possess an animal for a number of reasons. Most often, the shaman wishes to make use of the animal's particular abilities – in the case of a wolf, its fleetness of foot and heightened senses – in order to travel quickly, scout an area, or convey a message. Less often but more dangerously, an unscrupulous shaman may use a wolf to commit violence against those who have offended him or her.

Spontaneous astral projection and possession is rare, and normally indicates a significant latent talent. If the talented individual is not taken in hand by a trained shaman and taught how to control the gift, a great deal of confusion and damage can result. As the unskilled and often panicked astral traveler attempts to control what can seem like a dream, the host animal will often start to behave unpredictably, moving outside its normal hunting range and even attacking livestock, pets, and humans it encounters.

OPPOSITE

Since the 1960s, shamanic werewolves have spread from isolated native communities into New Age and neo-pagan groups across the world. Many are involved in environmental activism and ecoterrorism, especially where forests and other wild places are threatened. Corporations involved in logging and land development have placed particular emphasis on anti-werewolf security measures since the 1993 Clayoquot protests in British Columbia, when a remote camp was attacked by a werewolf pack reported to be more than 20 strong.

Private security contractors like Vindicorp in the U.S.A., Allecto in the UK, and Kronos in Germany have developed specialist anti-werewolf divisions, often recruiting veterans of military units like the 34th Specialist Infantry and Britain's Talbot Group. Security industry analysts have flagged supernatural threat assessment and management as a significant growth area over the next decade.

The 'Wolf Dance' of the Kaviagamutes. This Eskimo tribe was renowned for producing shamanic werewolves in the 19th century. (Library of Congress)

Identification and Threat

Almost all trained shamans forge strong ties to their home area and to the animal and other spirits that dwell there. They are seldom, if ever, active outside their home range, and in traditional societies their neighbors almost always know who the shamans are.

The strongest indicator that a case of lycanthropy is shamanic in nature is the fact that the human body remains behind in a deep, coma-like sleep. Experienced shamans know that their abandoned bodies are highly vulnerable while in this state, and usually take great pains to ensure their safety.

So long as a possessed animal continues to act normally, it is almost impossible to determine whether it is a shamanic werewolf or a normal wolf. It takes a trained shaman to recognize another shaman inside the animal's body. There are some behavioral clues – leaving the pack and the home range and traveling in a straight line toward some apparent destination, for example – but these are seldom unambiguous.

By and large, shamanic werewolves are the least dangerous – and the least often detected – of all werewolf types; they simply carry out the shaman's business and return to being normal wolves. However, they can become a threat under certain circumstances.

A small bear, supposedly inhabited by a Siberian shaman. (Library of Congress)

The most common threat arises when an untrained talent accidentally possesses a wolf's body and panics. This is often complicated further by the wolf's spirit trying to keep control of its body and panicking in its turn. The wolf will be unpredictable and aggressive, lashing out at anyone who comes near and sometimes even snapping at its own limbs and tail as the two spirits fight. The best defense in this situation is to keep one's distance and wait for the situation to resolve itself.

A worse danger comes from an unscrupulous or offended shaman who uses the form of a wolf to spread fear or exact revenge. While this is a common motif in horror fiction, it is a far rarer occurrence in real life. In most shamanic traditions, individuals who are arrogant or vengeful are weeded out during the early stages of training. However, it has been known to happen.

Urban shamans are becoming increasingly common, and their behavior can differ significantly from that of traditional shamans. They are more likely to take wolves out of their natural habitat, and to become addicted to the "rush" of inhabiting the body of an animal with enhanced senses and superior physical abilities. They are also more likely than traditional shamans to act out of pride or anger, leaving fear and damage in their wake.

Elimination and Prevention

In cases of shamanic lycanthropy, the wolf's physical nature is unaffected by the presence of a human consciousness. The creature is just as vulnerable to weapons and other dangers as it is in its natural state. Silver bullets will wound it and wolfsbane will poison it, but their effects are no more deadly than usual and the creature shows no enhanced resistance to normal weapons.

The most effective response to a shamanic werewolf is to eject the human spirit from the wolf's body. Once this is accomplished, the wolf normally flees and the shaman can be dealt with. Killing the wolf will eject the shaman's

ANIMAL POSSESSION

Rarer than shamanic lycanthropy, but far from unknown, is the phenomenon of animal possession. In these cases, a human is possessed by the spirit of an animal – most often an apex predator like a wolf or bear. The human then moves and acts like the animal until the possession is thrown off.

It is far from certain how animal possession occurs. The members of some wolf cults actively seek to be possessed, but in most reported cases the phenomenon seems to be accidental and the animal spirit is surprised and panicked to find itself inside a human body and surrounded by human beings. It will often seek to escape, lashing out violently at anyone who tries to stop it.

To the untrained eye, animal possession can look a lot like obsessive lycanthropy, but in cases of animal possession it is less common for the human host to retain any memory of events that occurred while he or she was possessed.

spirit, as will non-lethal measures such as tasers and tranquilizer darts. It can also be accomplished non-violently by another shaman who is more powerful that the one inhabiting the wolf.

The greatest challenge in a case of shamanic lycanthropy is to identify the shaman, especially if he or she does not want to be found.

In traditional societies, where shamans practice openly and everyone knows a great deal about their neighbors, the list of suspects is normally a short one. However, it can be very difficult for outside agencies to gain the trust of a traditional community and persuade its members to cooperate in an investigation. Most often, the community deals with a rogue shaman in its own way – sometimes long before outside investigators even arrive on the scene.

It is a great deal harder to identify and locate a werewolf shaman in an urban setting. Many urban shamans – especially those from Anglo communities – are secretive about their activities and not well known to their neighbors. Many are semi-trained or entirely self-taught, and not all have the skill or even the desire to control their abilities.

Leads the Wolf, a shaman of the Crow Nation in the late 19th century, was a famous teacher and supposedly trained an entire generation of shamanic werewolves. (Library of Congress)

Another shaman can pick up a trace of the possessing shaman's spirit by examining a possessed wolf, and follow that trace back to its source. However, this technique is not always successful, especially if the werewolf shaman is more powerful than the tracking shaman. There are ways to mask one's identity, and there have even been cases where a werewolf shaman has launched psychic attacks from a possessed wolf in order to prevent discovery.

Overall, the most effective technique has been old-fashioned detective work. The culprit can usually be identified by examining the behavior of the possessed wolf, determining motive, and narrowing down a range of suspects. Once this has been accomplished, the shaman can be apprehended using standard techniques and equipment such as tasers and handcuffs.

Chapter 3 – Sorcerous Werewolves

The ability to shift into the form of an animal – often a cat, a hare, or various kinds of bird – was a well-known ability of witches in medieval Europe, and the transcripts of many European werewolf trials describe a similar process.

Some anthropologists believe that – in Europe at least – this kind of shapeshifting is derived from the shamanism of the Palaeolithic and Mesolithic eras, as were various other aspects of medieval and later witchcraft. Be that as it may, there is a very definite difference between the shamanic process described in the previous chapter and the sorcerous lycanthropy described in medieval trials.

Like other kinds of werewolves, shapeshifting witches were hunted down with great determination by medieval sheriffs and inquisitors. The European witch hysteria of the 16th and 17th centuries brought them to the brink of extinction. By the 19th century, they were almost unknown outside the remotest parts of Europe and the wildest, most untamed colonies. Over the last hundred years or so, though, sorcerous lycanthropy has made a comeback.

Interest in witchcraft and other forms of traditional magic has grown steadily since the publication of Margaret Murray's seminal book *The Witch-Cult in Western Europe* in 1921. Over the next 20 years, organizations like the German *Ahnenerbe*, the British Talbot Group, and the FXU (Field Experimental Unit) of the American Office of Strategic Services (OSS) researched shapeshifting and other forms of witchcraft to assess their possible strategic usefulness. In the 1960s, the dawning of the "Age of Aquarius" heralded a resurgence of civilian interest in traditional religions and magic, laying the foundation for the New Age and neo-pagan movements of recent decades.

Like viral lycanthropes, sorcerous lycanthropes can learn to control their shapeshifting and assume the hybrid "wolf man" form. This seems to be a fairly recent development, though, since the bipedal form is never mentioned in reports of sorcerous lycanthropy before the 20th century. It has even been suggested that shapeshifting witches were inspired to develop this form by its popularity in the werewolf movies of the 1930s and 1940s, which made the wolf man an iconic image capable of striking fear into people worldwide.

A contemporary depiction of the crimes, capture, and execution of Peter Stumpf, the "Werewolf of Bedburg," who ran amok in 16th century Germany. (Mary Evans)

Case Studies

Besançon, 1521

In December 1521, shepherds Pierre Burgot and Michel Verdun confessed before the Inquisitor-General of Besançon in eastern France that they had used a mysterious salve to become wolves. Burgot confessed that 19 years previously, while collecting his scattered flock after a storm, he encountered three black-clad horsemen riding black steeds. On the promise that he would recover all of his flock unharmed, Burgot renounced God and swore allegiance to the lead horseman, whom he assumed to be a demon and who gave his name as Moyset. He was inducted into a coven of warlocks, of which Verdun was also a member. The two confessed to killing several women and children, mating with she-wolves, and slaughtering livestock. Verdun was captured after being wounded while attacking a traveler in his wolf form. Following the wolf's trail, the traveler came to Verdun's hut and found the shepherd inside, with his wife bathing a wound that was identical to the one he had inflicted on the wolf.

Burgot and Verdun were executed along with a third werewolf named Philibert Montot. There is no record that their master Moyset was ever found.

Dole, 1572

One of the most celebrated European werewolf cases was that of Gilles Garnier, the "Werewolf of Dole." In late 1572, several children went missing or were found dead in and around the French town of Dole, not far from Besançon. One evening a group of workers came upon what they took to be a wolf, but turned out to be Garnier crouched over the body of a child.

At his trial, Garnier, a recluse who lived alone with his wife some distance from the town, testified that he had been having difficulty in feeding his wife and himself when he was approached by a "specter" that offered him an ointment that would turn him into a wolf, allowing him to hunt more easily. He confessed to killing and eating at least four children who were between the ages of 9 and 12, and he was burned at the stake on January 18, 1573.

Bedburg, 1589

Peter Stumpf (also spelled Stubbe, Stumpp, and otherwise by various writers) terrorized the area around Bedburg, near Cologne, and met a grisly fate even for an accused witch. English writer Richard Rowlands describes it in his 1605 book *A Restitution of Decayed Intelligence*:

> One *Peeter Stump* for being a *were-wolf,* and having killed thirteen children, two women, and one man; was at *Bedbur* not far from *Cullen* in the year 1589 put unto a very terrible death. The flesh of divers partes of his body was pulled out with hot iron tongs, his armes thighes & legges broke on a wheel, and his body lastly burnt. He dyed with very great remorce, desyring that his body might not be spared from any torment, so that his soule might be saved.

According to a pamphlet circulated in England in 1590:

> The Devill who sawe him [Stumpf] a fit instrument to perfourm mischeefe as a wicked fiend pleased with the desire of wrong and destruction, gave unto him a girdle which being put about him, he was straight transfourmed into the likenes of a greedy devouring woolf... And no sooner should he put off the same girdle, but presently he should apeere in his former shape, according to the proportion of a man.

The same pamphlet reports that Stumpf lived as a werewolf for 25 years, killing and eating both humans and livestock and evading all attempts to capture him. Finally, Stumpf found himself closely pursued and slipped off his girdle, resuming his human form in an attempt to deceive his pursuers. However, he was seen by one of the hunters and arrested.

Creation

Sorcerous lycanthropy depends on sympathetic magic, and the change of form cannot be achieved without specific ingredients. One is absolutely indispensable: a wolf skin, or a belt made from wolf skin. The second is a salve made of various ingredients, usually including psychoactive plants like belladonna and

In the medieval and early modern periods, werewolves are often associated with the stealing or killing of children. Modern research has revealed no special connection between werewolves and the kidnapping of children. (North Wind Picture Archives / Alamy)

OPPOSITE

Medieval inquisitors believed that all cases of lycanthropy were due to witchcraft, and the Catholic Church has yet to officially recognize the existence of viral werewolves. Despite this, the werewolf-hunting Order of St. Cuthbert has been active since at least 1760 under the aegis of the Inquisition.

Documents in the Vatican's archives include transcripts of hundreds of werewolf trials, most of them from Italy, France, and Germany between the 12th and 16th centuries. Some scholars believe there was a significant outbreak of lycanthropy in Western Europe at that time, but others disagree. The frequent witch-hunts of the period would naturally have led to a higher rate of werewolf detection. It may also be significant that almost all documented trials relate to cases of sorcerous lycanthropy, suggesting that other types of werewolf escaped the Inquisition's notice.

psilocybin mushrooms. The composition of this salve suggests that sorcerous lycanthropy involves hallucination rather than actual shapeshifting, but several centuries' worth of eyewitnesses have been absolutely certain that the werewolf changed his or her form, sometimes before their eyes.

While sorcerous lycanthropy does not require the same level of training and discipline as the shamanic variety, almost all reports agree that the technique is not an innate skill and the neophyte must be taught how to perform the change. In medieval trial transcripts, the accused werewolf has almost always been inducted into a coven or made a pact with a "dark stranger," who provides the salve and skin as well as instruction in the technique of shapeshifting.

Richard Rowlands has the following to say about the process of transformation:

> The *were-wolves* are certaine sorcerers, who having annoynted their bodyes, with an oyntment which they make by the instinct of the devil; and putting on a certaine enchanted girdel, do not only unto the view of others seeme as wolves, but to their own thinking have both the shape and nature of wolves, so long as they wear the said girdel. And they do dispose themselves as very wolves, in wurrying and killing.

Identification and Threat

The keys to sorcerous lycanthropy are the animal skin or belt and the salve. Subjects normally keep these well hidden, but a search of a suspect's house or the base of a werewolf coven will normally lead to their discovery.

A wolf pelt is essential for a cursed werewolf to be able to transform. (North Wind Picture Archives / Alamy)

If these items are discovered, they constitute conclusive proof that a case involves sorcerous lycanthropy rather than any other kind. Until that time, however, it is necessary to rely on traditional investigative techniques.

Like shamanic lycanthropes, wolf-witches tend to operate within a limited home range, especially if they are part of a coven. Neophytes are often dependent on their superiors for the transformation salve, and personal bonds between coven members tend to keep them together.

Within their home range, though, sorcerous lycanthropes can be as much of a threat as any other kind. Attacks are often limited to the working out of personal disputes with neighbors, employers, and other acquaintances, but they can become considerably more widespread and deadly if the group is ideologically motivated. In this case, targets may include religious groups and buildings, local government officials and their offices, and others.

Over the last two decades or so, loggers and land developers have become a frequent target of werewolf covens. The alignment of wicca and neo-paganism with the environmental movement has led to werewolves taking part in several documented acts of ecoterrorism, ranging from the intimidation of work crews and planning officials to sabotage, assault, and murder. There have also been well-documented attacks on the homes and churches of fundamentalist religious figures, politicians, CEOs, and others who are seen as leading members of "the 1 percent" and are also targeted by more conventional activist groups such as the Occupy movement.

Recent cooperation between activists, wiccans, and werewolf covens has led to this class of lycanthropy being upgraded to "most urgent" by many governments. Even as they officially deny the existence of witches and werewolves, governments and military contractors worldwide are actively developing equipment and tactics to identify and neutralize them.

Elimination and Prevention

Arguably the most important tactics used against wolf covens by governments around the world are infiltration and destabilization. In this respect, these groups are treated in much the same way as other activist and terrorist breeding grounds.

A contemporary depiction of the Werewolf of Ansbach, which terrorized the Principality of Ansbach in 1685. Most authorities cite this as the most famous historical example of a cursed werewolf, although a lack of evidence means it could have been sourcerous.

Deep-cover operations lasting several years are necessary to win the trust and acceptance of a werewolf coven, and this can be particularly challenging for the agents involved. However, at the time of writing the global success rate of this approach is still deemed high enough to be acceptable. Agents placed in allied groups and tasked with getting close to a werewolf coven and discovering its base of operation have proven to be more reliable than agents placed directly inside the coven itself. Some direct-approach agents never win their way into the coven, and some – a noticeably higher proportion than in similar operations elsewhere – "go native," betraying their commanders and becoming loyal members of the target group.

Sorcerous werewolves exhibit normal vulnerability to all types of weapons in all body forms. Standard police and SWAT equipment and tactics are usually effective in dealing with all but the most militant and heavily-armed covens. Trackers and dogs have been especially useful in tracing their movements and discovering their bases. Dog handlers report that a keen scent hound such as a bloodhound can track an individual through multiple shape changes.

The enhanced efficacy of silver against sorcerous werewolves is still debated. In addition to its known effectiveness against viral lycanthropes, folklore and anecdotal accounts worldwide suggest that a silver wound will also break shapeshifting magic and force a witch to assume his or her human form immediately. For human rights reasons it has not been possible to test this theory in the field, and members of the 34th Specialist Regiment I interviewed were careful neither to confirm nor deny rumors that they carry non-lethal silver birdshot ammunition into action against suspected werewolf covens.

Chapter 4 – Cursed Werewolves

While many victims of viral lycanthropy have described their condition as a curse, there are also a number of reports of werewolves being more literally cursed to lycanthropy, usually by angry gods and saints. For obvious reasons these tales come mainly from the Classical and medieval periods, but at least some of them have ramifications that continue to the present day.

A werewolf curse frequently affects an entire community or bloodline rather than an individual. Sometimes its effects are limited to a certain number of generations, or it can be lifted by specific acts of penance, but more often it cannot. It carries on down the centuries, reminding each successive generation of their ancestors' misdeeds.

The most significant difference between a werewolf curse and other forms of lycanthropy is that it does not affect all of its subjects all of the time. Normally one or two members of the cursed family or community are required to be werewolves at any given time; they remain in wolf form for a fixed number of years (seven and nine are the most common), and if they survive, they are restored to human form permanently when their term is over. Sometimes there is an additional condition,

An illustration of the hunting of the Werewolf of Ansbach. (GL Archive / Alamy)

normally to refrain from eating human flesh. Upon regaining human form, the cursed werewolf is replaced by another relative or neighbor.

Cursed werewolves normally have no control over their form, and cannot adopt the intermediate "wolf man" form: they spend the entire period of their curse as normal-seeming wolves. A cursed werewolf always retains full human intelligence – the better, one supposes, to retain a painful awareness of its condition and regret whatever actions resulted in the curse. In a few cases, it has been reported that cursed werewolves have retained some vestiges of human speech, the better to tell their cautionary tales to others. This may be no more than a storyteller's device, however, since the tales of talking werewolves are almost exclusively found in the lives of early saints and similar morality tales.

Case Studies

The Antaei

In his *Naturalis Historia* ("Natural History") the first-century Roman writer Pliny the Elder tells of a werewolf clan called the Antaei from the remote mountains of Arcadia in southern Greece. They seem unrelated to the Libyan giant Antaeus who was defeated by Hercules.

While Pliny does not mention how they became werewolves, the Antaei show all the signs of a bloodline cursed to lycanthropy. Every nine years, a man is chosen by lot to become a wolf. He hangs his clothing on a tree and swims across a sacred lake, assuming the form of a wolf when he reaches the far side. If he can refrain from eating human flesh for nine years, he regains human form by swimming back across the lake, where he takes his clothes down from the tree and resumes his human life. At all times, Pliny says, one member of the family must be transformed into a wolf.

Ireland, 5th century

A story about St. Patrick gives a good example of a lycanthropic curse. The *Kongs Skuggsjo*, a Norse book compiled about 1250, tells that in Ireland Patrick encountered:

> one great race more hostile to him than the other people that were in the land… And when he preached Christianity to them … they took this counsel, to howl at him like wolves. But when he saw that his message would succeed little with these people, then he became very wroth, and prayed God that He might avenge it on them by some judgment, that their descendants might for ever remember their disobedience. And great punishment and fit and very wonderful has since befallen their descendants; for it is said that all men who come from the race are always wolves at a certain time, and run in the woods and take food like wolves; and they are worse in that they have human reason,

Thankfully, the bite of a cursed werewolf is not infectious. Artwork by Hauke Kock.

for all their cunning, and such desire and greed for men as for other creatures. And it is said that some become so every seventh year, and are men during the interval. And some have it so long that they have seven years at once.

Ossory, Ireland, 9th–14th centuries

The 14th-century Irish *Book of Ballymote* mentions "the children of the wolf" who ravaged the ancient Kingdom of Ossory, which occupied the modern counties of Laouis and Kilkenny. The *Historia Brittonum* ("History of the Britons") of Nennius of Bangor, written in the 9th century, states that "The descendants of the Wolf are in Ossory," and tells at length of "certain men of the Celtic race who have a marvelous power which comes to them from their forebears… they can at will change themselves into the shape of wolves with sharp tearing teeth, and often thus transformed will they fall upon poor defenseless sheep." It is unusual for cursed werewolves to be able to change shape at will, and Nennius may have introduced this detail from some other werewolf tradition.

In his *Topographia Hibernica* ("Topography of Ireland") Gerald of Wales tells of a pair of werewolves, husband and wife, encountered by a traveling priest in Meath in 1182 or 1183. The husband explained that they came from Ossory, and that their people had been cursed by the 6th-century abbot (and later saint) Natalis of Kilmanagh. The curse condemned a man and a woman to wander as wolves for seven years, at the end of which, if they survived, they would regain their human form and be replaced as wolves by another couple. The werewolf humbly asked the priest to give his dying wife the last rites, pulling back her wolf-skin with one claw to reveal the body of an old woman beneath the fur. When the priest had done so, the werewolf thanked him kindly and sent him on his way with detailed directions for the rest of his journey.

Creation

Modern werewolf experts tend to agree that tales of divine curses belong to the realm of mythology rather than science. Yet the fact remains that there is a distinct form of lycanthropy that is consistent across a wide area and different from all other classes – leaving the question of how bloodlines and whole communities come to be affected by this specific form of lycanthropy.

At the time of writing, there are two competing theories on the origins of this type of werewolf. One holds that the myths arose to explain a strain of hereditary lycanthropy that was probably viral in origin. The other suggests that they are garbled folk-memories of now-extinct wolf-cults.

The Tyana Institute has sent DNA-collecting expeditions to both Arcadia and Ossory, under the guise of wildlife surveys. Neither expedition managed to locate any wolves, which are believed to have been hunted to extinction in Ireland around 1786 and have not been seen in Greece since the 1930s. DNA recovered from bones and skins is still being processed, but so far all the samples recovered have been identical to the DNA of normal wolves. Further analysis is ongoing.

Anthropologists from Miskatonic University in Massachusetts visited Arcadia in 1932. The expedition was headed by Professor Tyler M. Freeborn of the Department of Anthropology and archaeologist Dr Francis Morgan, and visited Mount Lykaion and other sites associated with early wolf-cults. Through interpreters, the Americans interviewed many older residents, collecting local folklore about the area and its wolves, but the expedition had to be cut short owing to the political instability that attended the abolition of the Greek monarchy and the birth of the Second Hellenic Republic.

The expedition's report was published by Miskatonic University Press in 1935, but the print run was just 250 copies and it is very hard to obtain today. Second-hand reports indicate that any local memory of a local werewolf clan has degenerated into a jumble of folktales similar to those from all across Europe. However, the papers of British classicist Humfrey Payne, now in the library of the British School at Athens, suggest that the local people "have long been accustomed to telling pretty tales to wealthy

LYCAON OF ARCADIA

Although it does not seem to be connected with the Antaei or any other Greek werewolves, this Classical myth contains one of the first recorded instances of a divine wolf curse.

According to Greek myth, Lycaon – whose name contains the Greek word *lukos*, meaning "wolf" – was the first king of Arcadia. He ruled at a time when gods still walked among mortals, and when Zeus came to visit him, he decided to test the god's reputed omniscience by serving him the roasted flesh of another guest. Zeus realized what his host had done and punished Lycaon by turning him into a wolf – the notorious devourer of human flesh – and killing his 50 sons with thunderbolts.

What became of Lycaon after he fled the god's wrath is unknown. It is not recorded that he survived as a wolf, or that his descendants became werewolves. However, the Greek geographer Pausanias states that "they say that ever since the time of Lycaon a man has been transformed into a wolf at the sacrifice to Zeus in Lycosura, but the change is not permanent. If the wolf abstains from eating human flesh he will return to human form after nine years, but if he has tasted human flesh he remains a beast forever."

The story of Lycaon bears several similarities to the cult of Lycaean Zeus, described by the Roman natural historian Pliny the Elder under its Latin name of Jupiter Lycaeus. It is discussed in a later chapter.

foreign visitors, while holding their own truths closely to themselves." During the Axis occupation of Greece in World War II, both Italian *Alpini* and German *Ahnenerbe* personnel reported frequent wolf encounters in and around Mount Lykaion.

IDENTIFICATION AND THREAT

Of all the different kinds of werewolves, cursed werewolves are both the hardest to identify and the least threatening. This has led many werewolf scholars to conclude that they do not exist.

Any reported wolf sightings in areas where the animals have long since become extinct are worth investigating, especially if the region is cut off from wild wolf populations by water (like Ireland) or by a narrow land bridge (like southern Greece). There are many such reports each year, along with reports of mysterious big cats, Bigfoot-like creatures, and other cryptids. Most werewolf study programs make a habit of monitoring cryptozoology websites and message boards for reports of wolf and werewolf sightings, although these sources contain a great deal of "noise" in the form of hoaxes, misidentifications and uninformed speculation.

When a sighting looks promising, a small research team is normally dispatched to the site to investigate further. Ideally, a pattern of sightings should be established over a period of a few weeks, but in the case of wolves and other large predators it is better to move quickly in the hope of arriving before local farmers and hunters track down and kill the creature. This urgency naturally leads to some time and resources being wasted on false alarms caused by feral dogs, coyotes, and the like.

For the most part, cursed werewolves behave in the same way as natural wolves while they are in wolf form. When their behavior differs, it is for the better, in human terms. Possessed of human intelligence, they are often reluctant to prey on their neighbors' flocks and restrict their hunting to deer and small game. Some individuals even patrol their families' fields and gardens, preying on rabbits and other pests that would otherwise damage the crops. In some communities, it is customary to help inexperienced, old, or infirm werewolves by putting out joints of meat by some landmark such as a hilltop cairn.

While their unique nature and the mystery of their origins make them of particular interest to scholars, cursed werewolves are classified "lowest threat" by almost every werewolf-hunting organization in the world.

Elimination and Prevention

In the tales of early saints from Ireland and elsewhere, a fixed-term werewolf curse is comparable to a Catholic period of penance, and can only be imposed by a saint. If the sufferer outlives the term of the curse, he or she is restored to human form safe and well, and usually in a more pious frame of mind. On the rare occasions where such a curse is broken, it is due to the intercession of another saint to whom the werewolf has told its story and expressed fitting repentance.

Physically, cursed werewolves seem identical to natural wolves, and have no special resistances or vulnerabilities. Therefore any equipment that is

Most researchers into werewolf lore agree that the story of Little Red Riding Hood was an old, German cautionary tale about the danger of lycanthropy.

A 16th-century illustration of the story of Lycaon.

effective in dealing with natural wolves can be used with equal effectiveness against cursed werewolves.

For the reasons already given, it is seldom necessary to use deadly force against a cursed werewolf. The vast majority of missions targeting this class of lycanthrope are to capture for study. Tracking and sedation are the primary tactics, although some circumstances may call for darting or netting from a helicopter.

By far the greatest threat to an operation against cursed werewolves comes from the local community rather than the werewolves themselves. Those relatives and neighbors who are aware of the werewolf's nature – some of whom may themselves have spent time as werewolves – are understandably reluctant to help capture or kill one of their own. Once they become aware of the mission's objectives they will frequently respond with passive non-cooperation, which can escalate to sabotage and even confrontation. More than one mission has had to be aborted in order to avoid an international incident.

Chapter 5 - Obsessive Werewolves

Obsessive lycanthropy is perhaps the most controversial form of the condition. There are some, like Sabine Baring-Gould, who believe that all werewolves are obsessives, and that stories of physical transformation are either narrative embellishments or metaphors referring to the sufferer's furious state. There are others who believe that it does not qualify as lycanthropy at all, but is instead a form of delusional psychosis or some other mental illness. Others still claim that it is a form of shamanic lycanthropy in which a human being is possessed by an aggressive wolf spirit. Montague Summers echoes the official Vatican line that these are cases of demonic possession.

In obsessive lycanthropy, only the werewolf's behavior changes. During an episode, the sufferer remains in human form but is convinced that he or she has turned into a wolf. The werewolf runs on all fours, howls, and attacks livestock, children, and occasionally adults. When the episode has passed, the werewolf's human senses return, often accompanied by physical exhaustion. In most cases the werewolf retains clear memories of his or her actions, and may express regret or remorse for them.

An artistic depiction of the dual nature of the werewolf. Obsessive werewolves are often mistakenly assumed to have split-personality disorder.

It is possible that there is more than one form of obsessive lycanthropy. Some sufferers have shown a fear of silver and become severely agitated at the time of the full moon, while others have not. It is quite possible, though, that this fear is informed by the sufferer's knowledge of werewolf lore and has nothing to do with the condition itself. In some individuals, the lycanthropic fit seems to be a response to fear, anger, or other stressors, like the emergence of a strong, protective "alter" in a case of multiple personality disorder.

Obsessive lycanthropy has been recognized at least since the 2nd century AD. The Alexandrian physician Paulus Aegineta described the condition as a form of melancholy due to an excess of black bile. At least some of the reports of Norse berserkers and *ulfhednar* match this form of lycanthropy, though there are many more that do not; it seems likely that the berserkers were a mixed group in which multiple forms of lycanthropy were present.

English lexicographer Randle Cotgrave's *Dictionarie of the French and English Tongues* (1611) defines a werewolf as "A mankind Wolfe; such a one as once being flesht on men and

RABIES

At least some medieval reports of lycanthropy seem to refer to cases of rabies. The name of this condition is taken from the Latin word for madness, and its symptoms are very similar to those described by Petrus Salius for lycanthropy: "Foam appears at the mouth, they tear with their teeth, bark like dogs or howl like wolves, grind their teeth, sweat, and convulse." Montague Summers points out that these symptoms also appear in the New Testament as signs of demonic possession.

Salius also notes that lycanthropes avoid water at all costs; another name for rabies is *hydrophobia*, Greek for fear of water. However, modern werewolf researchers have not observed any aversion to water among their test subjects, and the other similarities are broadly agreed to be coincidental.

children will rather starve than feed on any thing else; also, one that, possessed with an extreame, and strange melancholie, belevves he is turned Wolfe, and as a Wolfe behaves himselfe." It is interesting that Cotgrave links obsessive lycanthropy with cannibalism here. The transcripts of medieval werewolf trials include frequent references to eating human flesh, and the consequent loss of interest in all other meat.

In 1563, Dutch physician Johann Weyer wrote that werewolves suffered from an imbalance in their melancholic humor and listed the physical symptoms as paleness, a dry tongue and a great thirst, and sunken, dry eyes. In his book *Daemonologie* published in 1597, King James I of England (VI of Scotland) regards lycanthropy as a mundane ailment without any supernatural cause, blaming instead "an excess of melancholy … which causes some men to believe that they are wolves and to counterfeit the actions of these animals."

Today, clinical lycanthropy can be found in the *Diagnostic and Statistical Manual of Mental Disorders* (DSM) as "a cultural manifestation of schizophrenia" because of four key symptoms: delusions (the belief that the patient is an animal); hallucinations (the false sensation of being in animal form); disorganized speech (making animal sounds); and "grossly disorganized behavior" (acting as an animal rather than a human being).

While it is true that some forms of mental illness can manifest as obsessive lycanthropy, there is a long and detailed historical tradition that suggests it is not the only cause of this condition.

Case Studies

Clermont, France, 12th century

The English writer Gervase of Tilbury writes of an outlawed French soldier named Raimbaud de Poinet, who seems to have fallen into a depressed state during the course of his wanderings until falling prey to "a sore amaze, and he grew frantic being changed into a wolf, under which shape he marauded his own native village, so that the farmers and franklins in terror abandoned their cottages and manors, leaving them empty and tenantless. This fearsome wolf devoured children, and even older persons were attacked by the beast, which tore their flesh grievously with its keen and savage teeth."

Gervase gives us nothing from which we can tell what kind of werewolf Poinet was. The "sore amaze" suggests an obsessive werewolf, but the physical transformation rules this out.

Pavia, Italy, 1541

The 16th-century physician Job Fincelius records a classic case of obsessive lycanthropy which took place in Pavia, northern Italy, in 1541. When caught following a series of violent murders, the accused werewolf "assured his captors that the only difference... between himself and a natural wolf, was that in the true wolf the hair grew outward, while in him it struck inward." In both Germany and France, more than one accused werewolf suffered partial flaying as the authorities tried to test the truth of similar assertions.

A werewolf gargoyle from *La Cathédrale Notre-Dame de l'Annonciation de Moulins*. While the Catholic Church officially denies the existence of werewolves, gargoyles such as this argue otherwise.

Creation

Obsessive lycanthropy can arise from a number of causes, both hereditary and otherwise. This has led many werewolf scholars to suggest that obsessive lycanthropy is nothing more than an umbrella term for a wide range of conditions that only manifest themselves in similar ways because of chance or cultural psychological stereotypes.

Genetic causes include neurological predisposition to obsessive and dysmorphic disorders, schizophrenic and schizoaffective disorders, and generalized psychosis. However, obsessive lycanthropy is only one of several conditions that can result from these predispositions. In almost all cases that have been analyzed by modern psychology, there is also something in the patient's early life that tips the balance toward lycanthropy and away from the others.

It is well documented that physical abuse in early childhood can lead to multiple personality disorders. While animal "alters" are not common, they are not unknown either, and a wolf makes a very effective defender of the fractured self. Dysmorphic disorders can lead to obsession with the strength, speed, beauty, and all-round capability of wolves,

This German woodcut from the 16th century is thought to be the oldest depiction of an obsessive werewolf. (Mary Evans)

which in turn can lead to obsessive lycanthropy as a form of wish fulfillment.

Serious anger management issues, regardless of their cause, can become identified with an animal power in the sufferer's mind, and this too can develop into a lycanthropic obsession. Some therapists believe that the animal self is a psychological construct; an alter ego, created to externalize the rage and to take the blame for the violence and destruction it causes away from the patient. In most Western cultures, the wolf has long been used as a symbol for animal ferocity and malevolence, so it is not surprising that this construct should take the form of a wolf.

Most controversial, though, is the proposition that some forms of obsessive lycanthropy occur when a human is possessed by an animal spirit, in a process that mirrors the normal course of shamanic lycanthropy. Some shamans can call upon animal powers at will, and it has been suggested that latent talents can do so spontaneously and unwittingly.

A few scholars of shamanism have also suggested that certain animals are born with a latent shamanic talent just as some humans are, but there is no general agreement on this. In order to confirm or rule out this proposition, it would be necessary to identify such an animal and gain its cooperation, and this has not yet been accomplished.

Obsessive werewolves don't really resemble wolves, but they often believe they do. (Mary Evans)

Identification and Threat

Obsessive werewolves are among the easiest lycanthropes to identify in the field. Because they do not transform, it is usually possible to identify them even in the midst of a lycanthropic episode. The face does distort a little under the accompanying emotional strain, but not sufficiently to defeat facial recognition software.

Eyewitnesses are also valuable in cases of obsessive lycanthropy. Acquaintances can readily identify the lycanthrope even in the midst of an episode, and even the most reclusive of obsessive lycanthropes cannot avoid developing a reputation in the local community. In developed countries, an obsessive lycanthrope will usually be known to local police and social services.

The uncontrolled violence of obsessive werewolves can make them a threat to local livestock and the local civilian population, especially the very young and the very old. However, a lone individual seldom poses a serious threat to well-prepared hunters.

Obsessive werewolves are most dangerous in groups, which can take the form of criminal gangs, "packs" that form spontaneously under a shared delusion, or organized cults. In these cases, the condition of each individual is strengthened by reinforcement from the rest of the group and can become as strong as any other form of psychological conditioning; group loyalty is usually very strong, and a group that has been together for any length of time will normally develop some level of tactical ability.

Elimination and Prevention

In dealing with a violent obsessive werewolf in the field, the most effective tools are the same as for subduing any violent suspect. Tasers will incapacitate the subject at close range so that handcuffs, straitjackets, or other restraints can be applied. At longer ranges and in dense cover, tranquilizing darts with a normal human dose will render the subject unconscious within a few minutes.

Where obsessive lycanthropy is purely psychological, it can be controlled by a combination of anti-psychotic medication and cognitive therapy. Where the individual has been part of a werewolf pack or cult, normal deprogramming techniques may also be required. The process can take months or years to complete and lifelong medication may be required.

If animal-spirit possession has been established, a course of instruction under an experienced shaman can help the individual come to terms with

BERSERKERS

Many descriptions of the Norse berserkers and *ulfhednar* mention howling, foaming at the mouth, and shield-biting without actual physical transformation, followed by exhaustion and weakness once the episode of *berserksgangr* has passed. These descriptions are completely consistent with obsessive lycanthropy, although other descriptions of *berserksgangr* vary. As will be discussed in later pages, the berserkers were clearly lycanthropes of various types who banded together, perhaps as members of a secret or forgotten wolf-cult.

Norse berserkers will be covered in greater detail in a later chapter.

their predisposition to possession, control spontaneous accessing of animal spirits, and build mental defenses against outside possession. Basic training can be accomplished in a few weeks, but lifelong practice is required to keep the threat at bay. Many spontaneous lycanthropes have developed into very capable shamans in this way.

A depiction of an 18th-century obsessive werewolf from Sweden. Since stories of werewolves were often used in centuries past to justify the actions of cannibals and serial killers, it is often difficult to determine actual accounts of an obsessive werewolf. (Mary Evans)

Chapter 6 – Werewolf Society

Lone Werewolves

Like wolves, werewolves are instinctively social beings, and the lone werewolf of horror literature and films reflects a small minority of actual cases of lycanthropy.

When a lone werewolf is encountered in the field, it is usually a newly infected viral werewolf. The individual was usually infected by accident, having survived an attack that was intended to be fatal, and has received no post-infection care or training. Ignorant, confused, and frightened, the werewolf becomes a solitary drifter, living on the move in order to avoid detection.

These untrained werewolves are usually a danger to themselves and others, transforming uncontrollably at the time of the full moon and unable to resist the instinct to attack humans and livestock. While they can be extremely dangerous when cornered, they pose a far greater threat by leaving human survivors who become werewolves in their turn. An outbreak can spiral out of control very rapidly if left unchecked.

A moody depiction of the isolation often experienced by werewolves, especially those recently infected with the virus. (Mary Evans)

A few shamanic werewolves live alone through choice, normally choosing remote locations in sparsely inhabited forests or mountains. These individuals are usually more shaman than werewolf, using a number of animal avatars and with no particular preference for wolves. Shamans who favor the wolf form tend to form packs of their own, or associate with wild wolf packs, preferring remote locations in both cases. In recent decades, though, some urban shamans have formed packs in a few of the larger cities, including San Francisco, Seattle, and Portland, Oregon.

Wandering Packs

Wandering packs are often based on human groups like biker gangs and mercenary groups. A few bands of New Age travelers have included werewolves, including some who claim descent from the ancient Irish Kingdom of Ossory.

The use of wolf imagery on unit and club badges is common among wandering packs, but is not exclusive to werewolf groups; a number of purely human motorcycle clubs and paramilitary units have adopted wolf – and werewolf – related names and iconography.

Most wandering packs started as human groups who came into accidental contact with lycanthropy and now treat their condition as another tool in their repertoire. It is not uncommon for the werewolves to form the elite inner circle of a group that is mainly human, and to expose human members to lycanthropy as part of a promotion ritual. Levels of post-infection care and training can be high, with an emphasis on pack loyalty.

The threat posed by wandering packs depends on their chosen lifestyle. Biker gangs can be rowdy and disputes frequently turn violent; paramilitaries are deadly by nature and sometimes ignore rules of engagement and chain of command; even normally peaceful travelers are well able to stand up against a society that is often hostile toward them. These human tendencies are often amplified in werewolves. When confronted by hunters or law enforcement, wandering packs can be among the most dangerous werewolf groups.

Urban Werewolves

Urban werewolves have existed since Roman times, but they have become a phenomenon over the last 50 years. They are often groups of young urban professionals who hunt in city parks and nearby wilderness areas. Most are viral lycanthropes, but there are mixed packs whose members include urban shamans, neo-pagan wolf-dreamers, and other types. There have also been reports of werewolf packs operating as street gangs, and of criminal gangs using werewolves as enforcers.

Most urban werewolves actually do their best to blend into society, though there are a few who seem to flaunt their lycanthropy by either appearing in public in their wolf man form, performing on stage, or even joining their high-school basketball team. (INTERFOTO / Alamy)

Territory is very important to urban werewolves, and most urban packs operate within a well-defined area. Territorial disputes with other packs are usually resolved by negotiation, but they can escalate into a full-blown turf war like the Chicago incident of 2006, when a platoon of the 34th was sent to support and advise Chicago SWAT and the Illinois National Guard.

Barring territorial disputes, an urban werewolf pack can be a good thing. The Talbot Group and the Tyana Institute have both reported that crime drops significantly when a werewolf pack moves into a territory, and anecdotal evidence also suggests that local populations of rats, coyotes, and strays are also reduced, with a corresponding boost to public health.

Urban werewolf packs generally take great pains to train and support new members, limit their hunting to less-frequented areas, and avoid interaction with humans. They also deal effectively with outside werewolves, vampires, and other supernatural threats that wander into their territory. Although the number and size of urban packs increases year on year, the majority are still categorized as a low threat.

Many regard "urban werewolf" as too much of a generalization to be useful. Even in mixed packs, werewolves distinguish between viral, shamanic, and other types of lycanthrope, tolerating the differences but remaining aware of them. Urban-professional packs see themselves as having nothing in common with gang-related "werebangers" – who, in their turn, frequently express their contempt in terms like "LAWYs" ("Law-abiding werewolf yuppies"), "Fidos," "Baltos" (a reference to the half-wolf sled dog immortalized in a 1995 animated movie), and "White Fangs."

Law enforcement officials tend to agree, lumping werebangers and other lycanthropic criminals in with werewolf motorcycle gangs and the more antisocial wolf-cultists under the term "Charlie Sierra" (criminal shapeshifter). They generally fall under the purview of gang and organized crime units, which are gradually receiving specialized anti-werewolf training. When I was at Fort Bragg interviewing members of the 34th for this book, a group of SWAT officers from various midwestern police departments was on base for a one-week course in Lycanthrope Identification, Classification, and Countermeasures, known informally as "Pooches for Pigs."

Rural and Wilderness Packs

The earliest reports of lycanthropy always came from remote areas, and even today a great many werewolf packs prefer to live far from human habitations. There are many good reasons for doing so: urban werewolves run a constant risk of discovery which can lead to hysteria and mob violence; newly infected lycanthropes are less able to control their condition, and may injure or kill innocent bystanders; and many werewolves have an instinctive love of the wild and are uncomfortable in an urban or suburban environment.

Not surprisingly, rural and wilderness packs are more likely than others to have close ties with neighboring packs of wild wolves. A few individuals, usually accidental lycanthropes, integrate into wild packs, often rising to high rank on account of their size, strength, and intelligence.

Rumors of wolf-werewolf hybrids, often with shapeshifting abilities of their own, go back for millennia but have never been scientifically proven. This has not stopped some members of the environmental movement calling for the extermination of all werewolves on the grounds that interbreeding will "pollute" the wild wolf population with "invasive human DNA."

Opinion on rural and wilderness packs is sharply divided. The FBI, the Tyana Institute and the Nightmen all regard them as the least harmful of all lycanthropes because they seldom stray outside their home range and pose little or no threat to humans. Local farmers and Department of Fish and

OVERLEAF:
Like their wild counterparts, werewolves preferred remote forest and mountain areas until a few decades ago. Since the late 1980s, however, there has been a significant rise in the urban werewolf population.

Some urban werewolves try to avoid detection, hunting in nearby parks and wilderness areas and living normal human lives between full moons. Others are more aggressive, often embracing a criminal lifestyle and working as enforcers for gangs and organized crime syndicates. A few become vigilantes, like the so-called "Wolf Girl of Seattle" who has been credited with several attacks on drug and human trafficking operations in the city since 2011. A local crime family has reportedly placed a million-dollar bounty on the Wolf Girl's head.

Wildlife officials take a different view because of their predation on livestock and wildlife. For the most part, though, organized werewolf hunts are rare.

Werewolf Cults

The vast majority of European wolf-cults were destroyed during the witch-hunts of the 16th and 17th centuries. A few have resurfaced since then, and some have survived in other parts of the world. However, most currently-active wolf-cults are much younger. Some were founded in the early 20th century, which saw a resurgence of mystical thinking across the west. Others have sprung up alongside the growth of New Age and neo-pagan groups in the last few decades.

Lycaean Zeus

Mount Lykaion is in the remote mountain region of Arcadia in southern Greece. The region figures heavily in many ancient reports of lycanthropy, and documents in the archives of the Tyana Institute suggest that in Classical times it was the home of a tribe of hereditary werewolves, perhaps descended from the semi-mythical Lycaon.

The cult of Lycaean Zeus involved human sacrifice, and may be very ancient in origin; in a paper on ancient lycanthropy preserved in the Institute's archives, Benjamin Franklin wonders whether the cult's original bloodthirsty deity was conflated with Olympian Zeus later in the Classical period. Greek and Roman writers regularly referred to ancient and foreign deities by the names of their own "true" gods.

An 18th-century illustration of the story of Lycaon.

Among the papers of Margaret Murray, preserved at University College, London, are extensive notes on lycanthropy. They date to the time when Murray was researching her celebrated book *The Witch-Cult in Western Europe*, and suggest that she was planning a chapter on wolf-cults and werewolves that never appeared in the published work.

Murray thought that the wolf-cult was either an offshoot of the witch-cult or an older, shamanic-animist religion that appeased the spirits of predatory animals with human and animal sacrifices; this suspicion has been borne out by modern archaeology, which has dated the earliest ritual activity on Mount Lykaion to the beginning of the third millennium BC. Murray's notes contain references to some darker traditions involving ritual cannibalism as a rite of passage for young men, although she dismisses reports of lycanthropic transformation following the ritual meal as delusions brought on by some hallucinogenic drug.

Some researchers argue that cursed werewolves appear more wolf-like when in their wolf man form than do viral werewolves, though no systematic study has yet been attempted. Artwork by Hauke Kock.

The cult seems to have survived the Turkish occupation of Greece, and grown through the 1920s. Nazi werewolf researchers investigated the area in the 1940s, as will be seen in a later chapter, and Greece's Axis occupiers were never able to subdue Arcadia completely.

Postwar emigration took the cult of Lycaean Zeus to North America, Australia, and many other countries, where it survives in secret. The cult seems very wary of exposure, and some scholars take this as an indication that it continues its cannibalistic ritual feasts. A handful of convicted cannibal killers have made statements referring to the ancient cult, but in all cases they were lone killers who became obsessive lycanthropes after reading

Close-up of a carved relief of Wepwawet from the Karnak Temple at Luxor, Egypt.

about the cult in Pliny or other sources. None has been firmly linked to the cult itself.

The cult of Lycaean Zeus is classified as an unknown threat by the Tyana Institute. At the time of writing, no agent has returned from a mission to locate and infiltrate the cult, and all are presumed dead.

Wepwawet

The Egyptian god Wepwawet, sometimes called "the opener of the way," is occasionally confused with jackal-headed Anubis, but hieroglyphic inscriptions speak of wolf-headed Wepwawet as a war-god who "opens the way to victory."

The Egyptian cult of Wepwawet became extinct in ancient times. Some scholars have taken the name "opener of the way" to imply that Wepwawet was a patron of military scouts, and researchers working for the Talbot Group in the 1940s speculated on the existence of werewolf scouts in the armies of Ramses II, but the nature of the cult remains unclear.

The worship of Wepwawet was revived in Britain and France in the 1890s. Initially popular only among intellectuals, it spread to the military of both nations before the start of World War I and even gained some adherents in Germany. Since then it has spread across the world, especially among assassins and special forces troops.

Unlike the cult of Lycaean Zeus, the modern cult of Wepwawet does not include cannibalism among its rituals. Burned offerings of meat are made to the god, usually in an underground temple. The Talbot Group and the Tyana Institute both believe that cult members can shapeshift into wolf form, and some reports suggest that they have other supernatural abilities including speed, silence, and invisibility.

The cult does not seem to have any defined agenda beyond the empowerment and advancement of its members. It has not been linked to any political assassinations or manipulation of government or army policies, or to any violent incidents of lycanthropy. The Tyana Institute classifies it as "generally benign."

Fenrir

In Norse myth, Fenrir is a monstrous wolf who is fated to kill Odin at the world-ending battle of Ragnarok. There is no indication that the Vikings worshiped Fenrir, and the Norse neo-pagan Asatru movement does not recognize Fenrir among its deities. The 19th-century Danish psychologist and mythologist Morten Lindegaard believed that Fenrir, Jormungand, Loki, and others were folk-memories of older, more savage gods that were supplanted by the Aesir and Vanir of Norse myth, but remained in the mythology as devil-like figures.

The present-day cult of Fenrir apparently dates back no further than 1933, when events in Germany inspired the growth of Nordic nationalism and fascist politics across Scandinavia. Fenrir was adopted as a patron by some of the more violent pro-Nazi groups in both Norway and Denmark, and his cult was particularly strong in the SS *Wiking* Division, which was recruited mainly from pro-Nazi Scandinavians.

The cult of Fenrir spread within the SS and documents recovered by US intelligence officers suggest that at least some of the SS *Werwolf* troops were members. The cult went underground at the end of World War II but has been growing in recent years, especially among white-supremacist groups that make extensive use of Norse and Nazi symbolism.

The cult's rituals almost always involved tests of strength and ferocity. They included armed and unarmed combats, ritual blood-letting, and the hunting of both human and animal prey. In return for blood-sacrifice, it was believed that Fenrir would grant the cultists strength and ruthlessness in order to defeat their enemies. Weakness was not tolerated, and cultists who failed any test of strength or endurance were hunted down and killed by their former comrades.

Not all Fenrir cultists were werewolves, but in 1946 former SS werewolves staged a bloody coup which left them in control. Today, the cult is a two-level organization consisting of werewolf "officers" and human "prospects" who undergo a series of tests and initiations before being exposed to lycanthropy.

The cult of Fenrir appears on a number of watch lists, but is generally regarded as too small and scattered to pose a serious threat beyond the local level. Its effectiveness is undermined by regular and bloody territorial disputes and power struggles. However, all concerned agencies agree if a leader should arise who is strong enough to unite its widespread chapters into a single cohesive force, it could become much more dangerous.

It should be noted that there is no connection between the present-day cult of Fenrir and the so-called "Children of Fenris," a short-lived cult that was active in Paris between 1919 and 1921, when it was destroyed by the Sûreté. The latter was a militant nihilist-anarchist group inspired by the carnage of World War I to bring about the Apocalypse. Despite the savagery of many of their actions, there is no evidence that any of the Children of Fenris were werewolves.

A werewolf berserker, shown on a Swedish bronze plaque from the pre-Viking Vendel period (AD 550–790).

The story William of Palermo, sometimes called "William the Werewolf" is a 14th-century French romance that features a "good" cursed werewolf. (Ivy Close Images / Alamy)

Chapter 7 – Werewolves at War

The Nazi *Werwulf* commandos are the best-known lycanthropic military force today, but they were by no means the first. Rulers and military leaders have always valued werewolves for their strength and aggression, as well as for the superstitious awe they inspire in an enemy. The use of werewolves as shock troops and elite guards goes back to the earliest times.

Lupi Dacii

The Twelve Caesars by Gaius Suetonius is still consulted by classicists today. It contains a wealth of detail about the lives of the first Roman emperors, from Julius Caesar to Domitian. Few know about the thirteenth book, covering the life of Trajan, which was expurgated by the Vatican in the 13th century. Only one copy of the complete work is known to exist today, hidden in a secret Vatican archive in the Castel Sant'Angelo in Rome.

As secretary and chief archivist to Trajan's successor Hadrian, Suetonius had access to first-hand accounts of the Dacian Wars, including reports of what he called the *lupi dacii* ("Dacian wolves") who wrought havoc with terrifying night attacks on Roman camps. Reading between the lines of Suetonius' account, the Dacians apparently had an elite force of werewolves – perhaps a warrior lodge, although details of Dacian society and customs are scanty – that served their kings as commandos and shock troops.

Nothing is known of the *lupi dacii* apart from the fact of their existence. All other details have been lost to the Vatican's determination to stamp out belief in werewolves throughout Christendom.

Wulfings, Berserkers and Ulfhednar

The Vikings were among the earliest people to incorporate werewolves into their military forces. King Harald Fairhair of Norway (*c.* 850–932) maintained a corps of berserkers called *ulfhednar* ("wolf-hide men") as shock troops in his campaigns to unify Norway, and many chroniclers of the time attest to their effectiveness on the battlefield.

Early in his reign, Harald's armies reached the region of Östergötland ("East Goth-Land") in present-day Sweden. This was a small kingdom whose ruling clan, the Wulfings ("Wolf People"), is mentioned in *Beowulf* as well as in various Scandinavian royal sagas. Swedish academic Bram Eldarsson has suggested that Östergötland was the home to an ancient werewolf bloodline from which Harald recruited his *ulfhednar* for his later campaigns.

Later Scandinavian kings followed Harald's lead, recruiting berserkers as elite troops or personal bodyguards. Accounts of the battle of Maldon in AD 991 mention *waelwulfas* ("slaughter-wolves") among the attacking Danish Army.

The nature of the *ulfhednar* and other wolf-berserkers is debated. Many scholars believe that the earliest berserkers were true werewolves descended from the Wulfing bloodline. As time went on, though, they were joined by wolf cultists and others who were attracted by their fierce reputation and their life of violent adventure. By the 11th century, the meaning of the word berserker had broadened to include wandering bands of brigands and a class of professional duelists comparable to the gunslingers of the Old West.

As Christianity spread throughout Scandinavia in the 11th and 12th centuries, various rulers issued decrees outlawing berserkers, and by the end of the Northern Crusades around 1290 werewolves were seen as agents of evil, just as they were in southern and Western Europe.

Ottoman Kurt Suçlular

In 1389 the Ottoman Army began to conscript light troops called *azab* to support the janissaries and other regular units. Officially named *Başıbozuk* ("irregulars") and known informally as *Delibaş* ("crazy heads"), these troops were recruited from the empire's criminal classes. They were used primarily as

OVERLEAF:
Although the Norse word berserker means "bear-skinned," King Harold Fairhair employed a corps of ulfhednar ("wolf-skinned") berserkers as shock troops and bodyguards in his conquest of Norway and his campaigns in Sweden. Some historians believe these werewolf warriors were the descendants of the Wulfing clan mentioned in *Beowulf* and other sources, which ruled East Gotland in the 5th century.

Later Viking rulers also used werewolf troops. An Anglo-Saxon poem describing the Battle of Maldon in 991 tells of *waelfulfas* ("slaughter-wolves") among the Viking force.

Early Christian saints condemned lycanthropy, and the practice died out after the Northern Crusades of the 12th and 13th centuries imposed Christianity on Scandinavia. Livonia (modern Latvia and Lithuania) was one of the last areas to be subdued, and lycanthropy was common among Livonia's noble families until at least the 16th century.

cannon fodder, but the most violent were organized into bands of varying size and used as shock troops.

Werewolves had been a thorn in the side of the Ottomans ever since Vlad Tepes of Wallachia began using them as raiders and skirmishers in his campaigns of 1459–62 against Sultan Mehmed II. Transylvania's Bathory dynasty, which had links to Vlad's family through the Hungarian Order of the Dragon, quickly followed suit, and for a while it seemed that all of eastern Europe might throw off Ottoman rule. Romanian historian Dr Radu Lupescu believes that Constantinople's werewolf infestation of 1542 was an attempt by Radu VII Paisie of Wallachia to revive Vlad's tactics, but this claim remains controversial.

After the werewolf hunt of 1542, Suleiman the Magnificent offered captured werewolves the choice of execution or service in the *Başıbozuk* as *kurt suçlular* ("wolf criminals"). Chroniclers from Hungary to Iraq write of the terror these lycanthropic troops spread on the battlefield, and on more than one occasion their mere presence was enough to shatter the morale of an opposing army.

The first *kurt suçlular* were recruited from the survivors of the 1542 purge and from the hills of Anatolia. This first draft was quickly supplemented from Transylvania, Wallachia, and Moldavia, which Suleiman had conquered by 1541. His campaigns against the Persian Safavid Empire in Georgia enabled him to strengthen the *kurt suçlular* with Georgian *vakhtang* werewolves, and his armies seemed unstoppable. However, Safavid leader Shah Tahmasp I, who still controlled eastern Georgia, was working to strengthen the Persian military in the face of Ottoman expansion. Tahmasp recruited *vakhtang* of his own. The battle of Erzurum in 1555 was a rare occasion when werewolves faced werewolves on the battlefield; the same year, the Peace of Amasya defined the borders of the Ottoman and Safavid empires for the next 20 years.

The *kurt suçlular* continued as a part of the Ottoman military through the empire's zenith and decline. The Wallachian Revolution of 1848 saw werewolves fighting on both sides, and among the Crimean War trophies stored beneath St. Petersburg's Artillery Museum is a large wolf-skin said to have been taken from a Turkish werewolf at the battle of Balaclava. Reported sightings of wolf-headed soldiers at the battle of Gallipoli in World War I are dismissed in an official British report preserved in the Imperial War Museum.

Today, Turkey officially denies using werewolves in any military or paramilitary force. However, conflicting reports from Kurdistan suggest that the *kurt suçlular* or their successors are still active in counterinsurgency and counterterror operations, and may be responsible for several alleged atrocities.

The Tyana Rangers

The Patriot militia known as the Tyana Rangers came out of a 1775 meeting between Benjamin Franklin and Ethan Allen. After capturing Fort Ticonderoga, Crown Point, and Fort George in New York, Allen's Green Mountain Boys had been driven from St. John's in Quebec (now Saint-Jeansur-Richelieu) by a pack of Loyalist werewolves that had been terrorizing the area to discourage the French-speaking Québècois from joining the American colonies in their rebellion against British rule. Frustrated by this defeat, Allen traveled to Philadelphia to consult with the Tyana Institute.

The combination of Allen's expertise in irregular warfare and Franklin's knowledge of the supernatural produced the improvements in equipment and tactics that the Green Mountain Boys needed, and it had another result as well. Inspired by his meeting with Allen, Franklin set about recruiting a specialist militia for dealing with British Freemasons, werewolves, and other supernatural foes.

As well as seasoned scouts, monster-hunters, and magical adepts, Franklin recruited a small group of werewolves as scouts and skirmishers. Using their wolf forms to evade British scouts and sentries, the werewolves – known as Randall's Volunteers for their leader, Lieutenant William Randall – brought back valuable intelligence on British movements and troop strength, destroyed British scouting parties and raided supply convoys.

The Tyana Rangers' most celebrated action, however, took place on December 25 and 26, 1776. A letter from Washington to Lt. Randall, preserved in the archives of the 34th Specialist Regiment, reads as follows:

> I cannot let this occasion pass, without conveying to you and your command my deepest congratulations and thanks, for your contribution to the recent action at Trenton. Your timely warning of the Hessians' necromantic preparations, and the valor displayed by your Volunteers, and the whole of the Tyana Rangers, in the action that followed, places the Continental Army, and the whole cause of Freedom, profoundly in your debt.
>
> I regret extremely that these few words must be your only acknowledgement for now, and I hope sincerely that a more enlightened time will come, when the triumph of reason over superstitious fear will allow the world to know the entire truth. For nothing is more certain in my mind, but that had the Hessians been permitted to complete their design, innumerable Patriotic lives must surely have been lost to their monstrous revenant cavalry.

The *Wolfsangel*, a German heraldic device used as a badge by SS Wolfen units.

The Tyana Rangers were disbanded at the end of the war, but the names of Randall and other officers appear in accounts of the Second Cherokee War and the War of 1812. They also took part in various anti-piracy actions around the Caribbean between 1791 and 1825, and in the Haitian Revolution of 1791–1804.

Wolf Partisans

As Nazi power extended across central and southern Europe, German troops found themselves under attack from partisans of all types, including werewolves. Transylvania was ruled by German allies and almost no activity was reported there, but werewolf attacks on Axis troops in Greece, Macedonia, and Bulgaria prompted the German *Ahnenerbe* to investigate.

Greece was occupied by the Axis powers from April 1941 to October 1944. Although Arcadia fell within the Italian zone of occupation, the German *Ahnenerbe* sent three expeditions to Mount Lykaion. At the end of the war their reports were recovered by the British Operation *Surgeon* and passed to the Talbot Group.

After some negotiation the group shared them with Operation *Paperclip*, and they are now in the archives of the 34th Specialist Regiment. The reports of werewolf attacks and German-Italian reprisals informed the development of the regiment's standard anti-werewolf tactics, which are used to this day.

The first expedition took place in the spring of 1942 under the command of a young SS *Hauptmann* named Wilhelm Streiber. Contact was apparently lost after a handful of initial reports describing the region and setting out a proposed survey plan for Mount Lykaion and its surroundings. The expedition's disappearance was officially ascribed to partisan action.

The second expedition, in the fall of the same year, was commanded by Colonel Gerhard Brandner and accompanied by a full company of Waffen-SS troops from SS-Sonderkommando Waggner. Up to the time of writing, no reports from the Brandner expedition have been found – or at least, none have been made public. However, KGB documents recovered by the CIA during the Greek Civil War of 1946–49 included reports from Soviet-backed Communist partisans on several crates that "seemed to contain large and aggressive animals of an unconfirmed species" that were taken off the mountain by truck in early November 1942 and put on trains for Berlin.

Ahnenerbe documents from early 1943 refer to "five crates of supplies, transferred from Greece for Project Löns." This name does not crop up anywhere else, but it is worth noting that Hermann Löns was the author of a book titled *Der Wehrwolf* – a popular novel about a German guerilla band in the Thirty Years' War that became required reading in the later years of the Nazi regime. It is tempting to believe that Project Löns was a forerunner of the later *Werwulf* program, and that the Mount Lykaion expeditions were sent to capture live werewolves for research purposes.

Division Lüneberg

More detailed information on Division Lüneberg and the Nazi *Werwulf* program can be found in Kenneth Hite's *The Nazi Occult*, also in this series.

Greece was not the only country targeted by *Ahnenerbe* and *Sonderauftrag H* research teams. Expeditions were also sent to Croatia and Lithuania, and German scientists compared notes with their Japanese counterparts in the *Ryokuryukai* ("Green Dragon Society") research organization. Out of all this research came the SS Division Lüneberg.

OPPOSITE:
While the U.S. Army's encounters with Nazi werewolves are fairly well-documented, reports from Soviet forces have only become available fairly recently.

During the Upper Silesian Offensive of March 1945, troops of the Soviet 59th Army advancing through Czechoslovakia suffered repeated hit-and-run attacks from werewolf groups displaying Nazi insignia. The first such contact was with a scout platoon commanded by Lieutenant (later Major) Yevgeni Demidov. In his memoirs Demidov writes "We had, of course, been briefed on the SS Werewolves, but it seems no one on our side knew that there were actual werewolves among them. We were prepared to face desperate fascist insurgents amid the rubble of German towns – indeed, we were eager to reverse the roles of Stalingrad and felt our experience there had prepared us for anything the enemy might attempt. But this attack by supernatural beasts in the snowy terrain – for this, we were completely unprepared. I lost good men there, and I will never forget it."

On the surface, Lüneberg was a resistance organization established to carry out guerilla attacks on advancing Allied forces and thwart teams from the Monuments, Fine Arts, and Archives program (MFAA or "Monuments Men") and operations *Surgeon* and *Paperclip* so that artifacts, data – and in the end, personnel – could be spirited away to safety. A station named "Radio Werwolf" broadcast propaganda and sent coded messages to these groups.

Nazi Germany's true werewolves were concealed beneath the umbrella of this dispersed and compartmentalized organization. Their best-known action took place in Cologne in late May of 1945, when five SS *Wolfen* ambushed an MFAA team in the Lehrichstrasse near the city's famous cathedral. After a brief skirmish, troops from the 34th Specialist Regiment conducted a sweep of the old city which resulted in many casualties on both sides. *Wolfen* have also been implicated in war crimes in Russia, Poland, France, and Norway.

Initially located in Poland, Division Lüneberg's command and training facility was moved first to Thürenberg, Czechoslovakia and then to Schönsee, Bavaria, which was liberated by American troops on April 25, 1945. Officers from Operation *Paperclip* were able to retrieve a small quantity of papers from a burning building, which eventually found their way to Project Leash.

Modern Werewolf Forces

Since the end of World War II, many nations are known or believed to have experimented with lycanthropy as a part of various "super-soldier" initiatives. The most reliably documented projects and units are described below.

Project Leash: A successor to the FXU (Field Experimental Unit) of the wartime OSS, this CIA-run experiment was based on documents recovered from the Division Lüneberg facility at Schönsee and *Ryokuryukai* headquarters in Tokyo. Scrapped in 1948 after several test subjects from this and Allied projects escaped and fought with each other.

The Hidehira Project: Named for a 12th-century Japanese clan leader who was supposedly raised by wolves, the Hidehira Project at Nagano University is officially an attempt to clone the extinct Honshu wolf. However, the Tyana Institute has traced the bulk of the project's funding back to the Japanese Defense Agency and believes that the project's true goal is to create lycanthropes for military purposes, perhaps by gene-splicing.

Randall's Rangers: Reformed in 1947 and augmented by German research, this werewolf special forces group has served alongside the 34th Specialist Regiment, Delta Force, and the Navy SEALs in Korea, Vietnam, Iraq, and Afghanistan. The Rangers also scouted inside East Germany and western Russia between the loss of Gary Powers' U-2 spy plane in 1960 and the introduction of the SR-71 Blackbird in 1966.

L Company: A product of the Talbot Group's research, L Company is nominally attached to Britain's Royal Marine Commandos, but for all practical purposes it falls under the command of the Director Special Forces.

Its existence is officially denied by the Ministry of Defence, but L Company has seen action in Northern Ireland, the Falklands, Bosnia, and Afghanistan.

Karelia Division: Attached to the 45th Detached Reconnaissance Regiment of Russia's Spetsnaz GRU force, CIA sources suggest that despite its name the Karelia Division is no more than company strength. It seems to consist mostly of shamanic werewolves from Siberia, northern Russia and Lapland. This was the most successful line of Russian lycanthropy research after the United States beat Soviet forces to Schönsee. The Karelia Division has reportedly been active in Chechnya, Kosovo, and Ukraine in recent years.

Sayeret Zev: The United States shared its werewolf research with Israel as part of the 1978 Camp David Accords that normalized Israeli-Egyptian relations after the Yom Kippur War of 1973. Sayeret Zev is classified as a long-range reconnaissance force, but like many Sayeret units it conducts a wide range of antiterrorist and counterinsurgency operations both inside and outside Israel's borders.

Dağ Keşif Taburu (DKT): This branch of the Turkish OKK (Special Forces Command) is believed to be descended from the *kurt suçlular* founded by Suleiman the Magnificent. There are no reports of its activities prior to 2002, although rumors of wolf-related atrocities have been coming out of both Turkish and Iraqi Kurdistan for decades. The DKT has also been active along the Syrian border, and in various counterterrorist operations in eastern Anatolia.

Werewolf Paramilitaries

The existence of werewolf paramilitaries was not widely reported until The Hague war trials arising from the Bosnian War of 1992–95, when the Chetnik Wolves of Vučjak was named among several other groups. A Tyana Institute report for the US State Department confirmed that this group was entirely human, but flagged a number of other paramilitary groups worldwide as confirmed or potential werewolf threats.

Brothers of Fenrir: A neo-Nazi organization with ties to biker gangs and organized crime, the Brothers of Fenrir was apparently founded in Sweden in 2007. Since 2010, it has spread to Norway and Denmark, but attempts to establish a chapter in Iceland have been unsuccessful so far. The Brothers have been linked to attacks on immigrant communities and foreign-owned businesses and the intimidation of left-wing politicians. Sweden's SAPO security police classifies the group as growing and potentially dangerous.

Ossory Volunteers: A 1982 Royal Ulster Constabulary report named this group as a possible splinter wing of the Provisional IRA. Since the IRA ceased combat operations in 2005, the Ossory Volunteers have been linked with gun-running and assassinations in eastern Europe and North Africa. Terrorist communications intercepted by Britain's Government Communications Headquarters suggest that surviving members of the group are working as mercenaries in various trouble spots, including Chechnya and Ukraine.

Broken Mountain Republic: First reported by the FBI as a localized separatist-ecoterrorist group, the Broken Mountain Republic is based in northern Idaho and has been involved in attacks on state and federal law-enforcement facilities around the state. It claimed responsibility for the deaths of six Idaho Department of Fish and Game employees during a local wolf cull in 2014, although a local coroner ruled that the deaths were caused by large wolves.

Mureș Brigade: Allegedly active during the Transylvanian ethnic disturbances of 1990's "Black March," the Brigade is an ethnically Romanian militia dedicated to the expulsion of ethnic Hungarians from the country. It is believed to have links to the nationalist Romanian Hearth Union and sympathizers within both local and national government. The CIA is still assessing reports that some of its members fought in Bosnia as volunteers or mercenaries.

Hounds of God: A secret society of werewolves based in Latvia and Lithuania that traces its origins to the 11th century. Its stated purpose is to combat witches and other supernatural threats, but it was involved in nationalist uprisings against the Russian Empire, the Nazis, and the Soviet Union.

Chapter 8 - Other Were-Creatures

A pre-Columbian painting of a Nagual.

Werebears (Northern Europe)

The Old Norse word *berserker* translates literally as "bear-skin man," and contemporary descriptions of Norse armies include elite warriors dressed in bear skins as well as wolf skins. The Persian chronicler Ibn Miskawayh tells of a "great and terrible bear" that rampaged through the town of Bardha'a (modern Barda, Azerbaijan) when the city was sacked by the Rus in AD 943, "which fought with the strength of a bear and the intelligence of a man, and which the attackers said partook of the nature of both."

Werebears have always been less common than werewolves, but they are still to be found in the forests of northern Russia and Scandinavia, as well as in remoter parts of the United States and Canada. While werebears are normally reclusive and dangerous only when harassed, they have been known to associate with environmental activists in their home areas and to intimidate logging and construction crews. According to a 2011 report by the FBI's WSUB Section, fewer injuries and fatalities result from these incidents than from similar werewolf confrontations.

Skinwalkers (North America)

According to Native American legends, skinwalkers are witches – usually, but not always, male – who can transform into animals, including wolves. Especially well-documented in Navajo tradition, skinwalkers are universally regarded as evil and destructive.

Skinwalkers are similar to the shamanic werewolves of Europe in many ways, but also have some things in common with sorcerous werewolves. They are not limited to wolf form, but require an animal skin to affect their transformation. In human form, their eyes reflect light like an animal's, but in animal form their eyes are dead and lifeless. They are said to be unnaturally fast and agile, and almost impossible to catch. It is said that some Navajo skinwalkers can adopt the form of another human being, or possess another human being by making eye contact.

There are very few reports of skinwalkers being active outside of Reservation lands. They are active mostly at night, and have been known to attack houses and vehicles. While it is generally agreed that Navajo shamans have effective means of identifying and counteracting skinwalkers, the Navajo Nation has consistently refused to share its knowledge with outsiders, and skinwalker sightings are not generally reported.

Nagual (Central America)

The pre-Columbian word *nagual* is often translated as "shapeshifting witch," but the known abilities of the *nagual* are more consistent with shamanic lycanthropy. The ability to transform into a jaguar, puma, or other animal form is latent in individuals who are born on a day linked to the animal's spirit in the Mesoamerican calendar system, and can be developed and controlled through training and experience. Originally associated with Tezcatlipoca, the patron deity of change through conflict, *nagualism* was condemned as witchcraft by the Spanish, who regarded Tezcatlipoca as a demon of chaos. *Nagual* became synonymous with *bruja* ("witch"), and this attitude persists to the present day.

A *nagual* is not intrinsically good or evil, but acts according to his (or more rarely, her) personality. Many are valued by their communities, and are called upon to undo evil caused by others of their kind.

The existence of an elite order of Aztec "jaguar warriors" has been well established. According to a Jesuit report that is now in the Vatican's restricted archives, some of the jaguar warriors were shapeshifters. They were held in high esteem, and frequently acted as assault troops. There was said to be no evidence of shapeshifters in the companion order of "eagle warriors."

The Mexican intelligence agency CISEN has been tracking *naguals* and other paranormal threats since the Aztec Mummy crisis of the late 1950s. CISEN reports a marked increase in *nagual* activity beginning in 2008; they seem to be active on both sides of the drug war, and have been classified as a serious threat.

Mexican GAFE special forces troops have been training with the 34th at Fort Bragg since early 2009, and in February of 2014 the Mexican government officially denied rumors that the jaguar warriors have been revived as a secret army unit attached to the GAFE.

Buda (North and East Africa)

Buda is a form of witchcraft originating in North Africa, the Horn of Africa, and the Near East. Its powers include the evil eye (the power to injure or kill with a glance) and the ability to shapeshift into a hyena. It was first reported in 1406, in the *Hawayan Al-Koubra* of Al-Doumairy; French and English accounts from the 19th century broadly confirm Al-Doumairy's account of

The emblem of a Leopard Society preserved in the Brooklyn Museum. (Brooklyn Museum)

shapeshifting witches attacking sleepers and drinking their blood. In Sudan, Tanzania, and Morocco they are also accused of digging up graves and eating the corpses, a behavior that is not unknown in natural hyenas.

Because of *buda*'s many similarities to European and Middle Eastern witchcraft, the Tyana Institute classifies it as a form of sorcerous lycanthropy. Bipedal hybrid were-hyenas have been reported from western Sudan, and shapeshifting hyena cultists are active in Mali, Senegal, Guinea, and Burkina Faso.

The 34th Specialist Regiment classifies *buda* shapeshifters as a growing threat, especially in immigrant communities. A report on a string of mutilations among Sudanese immigrants in Omaha, Nebraska is pending, and the CIA's GUID (Global Unusual Incident Desk) is actively investigating claims that bipedal lycanthropes committed atrocities during the 2012 Mali coup led by General Amadou Sanogo. It is not yet clear whether they were acting as death squads for one side or the other, or simply taking advantage of the chaos.

Leopard Societies (West Africa)

Word of African leopard societies first reached Europe in the 19th century. Colonial officials of various European powers reported on murderous secret

A kitsume in the form of a nine-tailed fox.

societies whose members wore leopard masks and skins, and killed with steel claws or knives. There were also rumors of cult-like activity, cannibalism, and witchcraft.

Despite strenuous efforts to stamp them out, the leopard societies survived, growing stronger in the late 1940s when they allied themselves with many of the anti-British rebellions that flared up immediately after the end of World War II. Although official reports stress the use of masks and skins, a 1948 memorandum from the Talbot Group to the British Colonial Office stated that "it must be recognized that these secret societies, and others like them elsewhere in the British Empire and Commonwealth, include among their senior membership certain adepts who have the ability to become leopards rather than simply adopting a leopard disguise."

Leopard society activity has declined since the middle of the 20th century, although both the Talbot Group and the Tyana Institute believe the societies still exist. There have been unsubstantiated reports of leopard society assassins taking part in the Sierra Leone Civil War of 1991–2002, the Second Liberian Civil War of 1999–2003, and the First Ivorian Civil War of 2002–07. UNPAMON, the United Nations Paranormal Monitoring program, rates leopard societies as a serious threat in those three nations but reports no activity elsewhere.

Weretigers (South and East Asia)

Weretigers are found in India, China, and Southeast Asia. They are almost always described as violent killers with a taste for human flesh, and the overwhelming majority of reports over the last 200 years are consistent with shamanic or sorcerous lycanthropy. These creatures are invariably solitary, and are as strong and elusive as natural tigers.

An exception to the general pattern is the *harimau jadian* of Malaysia and Indonesia. Their lycanthropy passes down through certain bloodlines and is controlled by spells, fasting, and meditation. When in tiger form, the *harimau jadian* are benign creatures who kill wild pigs to protect the community's crops.

However, they can be dangerous. While in tiger form they can fail to recognize friends who do not greet them by name, often with fatal results. They have also been known to stalk and kill outsiders who wrong them or their community.

The archives of the 34th Specialist Regiment include translations of Japanese military reports dated from 1942–44 which describe contact with resistance groups from the Malayan People's Anti-Japanese Army, including stealthy night attacks by "tigers of unusual intelligence" that specifically targeted officers.

There are no records of weretigers being active outside their home range; the governments of both China and India officially deny that they ever existed. However, during the Indo-Pakistani War of 1971 and the standoff of 2001–02, the Pakistani Army brought in trackers and tiger experts from the Karachi Zoo after a spate of tiger attacks on officers in the field.

Hengeyokai (Japan)

Unlike Western lycanthropes, Japanese *hengeyokai* are animals, or animal spirits, which have the power to shift into human form. Japanese folktales tell of many varieties, but the following *hengeyokai* have been positively identified by the *Yokai Jingcha* (lit. "spirit police"), Japan's major paranormal investigation and enforcement agency.

Kitsune

Kitsune are fox spirits. Those who interact with humans are usually female. Younger *kitsune* are indistinguishable from foxes, but they grow additional tails as they age: the oldest and most powerful *kitsune* have nine tails.

The ability to shift into human form is gained between 50 and 100 years of age, and with practice a *kitsune* may become skilled enough to impersonate a specific person. Otherwise, the favorite form is that of an attractive young woman. While in human form, a *kitsune* may forget to hide its tail or neglect to change the form of its shadow, especially if drunk or distracted. Dogs provide the most reliable means of detection because they have an instinctive dislike of the creatures.

The *Yokai Jingcha* classifies *kitsune* as a minor threat since they are not usually violent. However, they delight in seducing and playing tricks on susceptible men, especially those they deem too self-important or bad-tempered. The *Yokai Jingcha* routinely investigates any scandals or humiliating accidents involving Japanese politicians or high-ranking executives.

Tanuki

The *tanuki* is a Japanese creature whose name is usually translated into English as "raccoon-dog." It is a small canid with raccoon-like eye markings. In former times, *tanuki* liked to impersonate Buddhist monks and tempt them into breaking their vows: food, drink, and female company were their favorite inducements. They also played tricks on travelers and humiliated those they regarded as strait-laced or overly pious.

These days, *tanuki* can be found in many Japanese cities operating successful restaurants and other small businesses related to food, drink, and entertainment. Like *kitsune*, they are regarded as a low-threat creature, although in 2009 the *Yokai Jingcha* did investigate a number of incidents in Tokyo's Shinjuku ward, including a restaurant inspector who was found lashed to a flagpole in his underwear and a *yakuza* collector whose loaded gun had to be surgically removed by a proctologist.

Tengu

Tengu are hawks, or sometimes crows, that inhabit remote wooded places. In human form, they often have long or hooked noses, which make them easy to distinguish from Japanese humans.

The *tengu* are easily provoked by a lack of respect for nature. Even petty offenses like littering can drive them into a rage. In former times they tolerated the presence of the ascetic *yamabushi* warrior-monks and even earned a reputation as expert swordsmen, but they normally have little tolerance for trespassers.

The *Yokai Jingcha* rates *tengu* as a serious but localized threat, and works with the Ministry of Agriculture, Forestry, and Fisheries to keep tourists away from known *tengu* territory. For the most part, this policy has been successful; however, in 2007 *Yokai Jingcha* response teams accompanied riot police and forest rangers onto the slopes of Mount Aino, west of Tokyo, after a party of Dutch mountaineers disappeared. Officially no remains were ever found, and the group is believed to have suffered a fatal mishap after wandering off the trail.

Kumiho (Korea)

Like the Japanese *kitsune*, the *kumiho* ("nine-tailed fox") of Korea is said to arise when a fox lives an exceptionally long life: in this case, a thousand years. However, recent studies funded by the Tyana Institute and carried out at the Kyung Hee University in Seoul have reached the conclusion that they are a local kind of sorcerous lycanthrope resulting from an ancient cannibal-cult. Documents from the Gojoseon period speak of *yeou manyeo* or "fox witches" stealing and eating children, which is the key element of most *kumiho* legends.

In August 2005, US intelligence sources reported a supposed "joint exercise" by North Korean troops and police in the mountains around Jonchon. A few days after the exercise, a woman was executed in Jonchon for the murder of a young boy and "unspeakable crimes" – thought to be a euphemistic reference to cannibalism. The same day, a government proclamation condemned as counter-revolutionary "the holding of superstitious beliefs, telling tales of witches and monsters, and speaking or behaving in a folkloric [sic] manner." While acknowledging the difficulty of obtaining reliable information from North Korea, the Tyana Institute has classified the Jonchon incident as a possible *kumiho* attack.

Chapter 9 – Werewolf Hunters

Werewolf hunters have existed throughout human history. Many groups are dedicated to protecting humanity from all kinds of supernatural threats, including werewolves. Some are made up of hunters and warriors who seek to measure their own prowess against this most dangerous of foes. Some seek to study werewolves and understand the condition of lycanthropy, either in the hope of developing a cure or to harness the power of the werewolf for human political and military ends.

Government and other documents studied up to the time of writing have identified the following organizations as being involved in werewolf hunting, lycanthropy research, or both. There are certain to be more such groups, still in the shadows.

Apollonius of Tyana for whom the Tyana Institute was named.

The Nightmen

Best known in recent years for its role in the Zombie Wars, the US Army's 34th Specialist Regiment has been involved in anti-werewolf actions in World War II and before. Its history goes back to the early days of the American Revolution, in which its predecessors faced a wide range of supernatural foes. Some were of native origin, and others were summoned and controlled by the sorcery of British and Loyalist Freemasons.

According to documents supplied by the 34th Specialist Regiment for a planned unit history, the Nightmen trace their ancestry to a Revolutionary War militia group called the Tyana Rangers. Whatever its ancestry, the present-day unit was formally organized in 1943 as part of the OSS.

Its initial brief was to provide troops trained in unconventional warfare for support roles in clandestine operations by the OSS and similar groups. As the war progressed and the Allied high command came to realize the extent of Nazi occult research, the 34th found itself increasingly called

upon as an occult warfare unit. With very few exceptions, it has remained in this role to the present day.

The 34th is based at Fort Bragg, North Carolina. Outside the Zombie Wars, elements of the 34th have seen action in Iraq, Somalia, Bosnia, and the Philippines. Company-strength detachments were sent to various parts of each conflict zone in response to reports of lycanthropes and other supernatural threats on the enemy side.

It is known that some retired personnel from the 34th are currently active in Bosnia-Herzegovina as private military contractors. Their official mission is to help local forces track down escaped war criminals, but there are persistent rumors that they and their hosts are training each other, sharing techniques of supernatural warfare. Similar exercises are said to have begun in Romania when that country became a full member of the European Union in 1997.

As a unit of the US Army, the 34th Specialist Regiment recruits exclusively from within the US military. The bulk of its personnel come from Army backgrounds, frequently with special forces experience, and have been transferred to the 34th after displaying both skill and courage in an encounter with a supernatural foe. A minority of the 34th's personnel is recruited from private military contractors with supernatural experience.

The structure and basic equipment of the 34th is typical of a US Army infantry unit. It also uses special equipment corresponding to the mission, such as nets, blessed or silver-dipped ammunition, and high-intensity, vehicle-mounted UV floodlights.

The Tyana Institute

The Tyana Institute has already been mentioned in connection with the 34th Specialist Regiment, but its involvement in paranormal warfare seems always to have been incidental to its main purpose. It was founded in 1753 at the College of Philadelphia with the aim of "advancing knowledge of natural philosophy," and one of its earliest patrons was Benjamin Franklin.

It is said that it was Franklin who gave the society its name, and perhaps its earliest impetus into the study of the paranormal. Apollonius of Tyana was a Greek philosopher with whose work Franklin was undoubtedly familiar: among his exploits, according to his biographer Philostratus of Athens, was the defeat of a vampiress who had been preying on one of his students.

Nominally based in Geneva, the Tyana Institute is descended from Franklin's society and devotes itself to the scientific study of vampires, werewolves, and other supernatural creatures. Its North American headquarters are in an anonymous building on the campus of the University of Pennsylvania. The Institute's membership is dispersed around the world, and includes some of the most distinguished zoologists, botanists, and taxonomists in contemporary academia.

The Institute has sponsored expeditions to Brazil, Vietnam and elsewhere in order to locate and record previously unknown plant and animal species. It has

OPPOSITE:
Founded shortly after the Russian Revolution, the Zaroff Society is the only group known to hunt werewolves and other supernatural creatures for sport rather than study or defense. Its founder General Mikhail Zaroff hunted werewolves in the forests of Livonia and the Transylvanian Alps, and his diaries describe them as "savage, cunning, and intelligent... certainly the worthiest adversaries I have yet hunted, and possibly the most dangerous game in the world."

Since Zaroff's disappearance in 1924, the Society has continued to respond to werewolf sightings around the globe. In recent decades, they have occasionally come into conflict with other groups who are hunting the same creatures for different reasons. Lt. Robert Whitney of the 34th Specialist Regiment describes them as "dangerous amateurs," while Col. Paul Montford of the Talbot Group was once challenged to a duel by, in his words, "a titled foreign idiot" whom he ordered away from a secured exercise location.

funded research projects at the more scientific fringes of cryptozoology, and there have always been rumors that some of its members take an interest in subjects like Bigfoot, lake monsters – and werewolves – rather too seriously for mainstream academic tastes.

While scattered and loose-knit, the membership of the Tyana Institute can be mobilized at surprisingly short notice. Funds are seldom a problem thanks to the Institute's patents on a number of plant-derived medications discovered by its members, and there is scarcely a reputable university anywhere in the world that does not contain a handful of Institute members or their correspondents.

Unlike most of the other groups listed in this chapter, the purpose of the Tyana Institute is study rather than defense. Its members will only kill a werewolf as a last resort, to protect themselves or others: capture is always the primary goal. An expedition organized by the Tyana Institute will look exactly like any other zoological expedition, traveling in locally acquired four-wheel-drive vehicles and carrying a great deal of scientific equipment. A few rifles and pistols, often personal property, are carried for self-defense, along with nets and high-powered dart rifles capable of delivering powerful doses of tranquilizers.

The Talbot Group

Nazi Germany was not the only power which tried to develop super-soldiers during World War II. In 1941, the assassination of a key scientist put a halt to a secret US Army project which aimed to develop super-soldiers using a strength-boosting serum.

That same year, a young Welshman attracted the interest of the London Controlling Section, a secret department within the British government. While the Section's official remit was to plan and execute strategic deceptions, it was also involved in supernatural warfare. Its members included Wing Commander Dennis Wheatley, who later became famous as an occultist and horror writer, and it has long been rumored that the magician Aleister "the Great Beast" Crowley was among Wheatley's agents. Following reports of lycanthropy near the village of Llanwelly, the London Controlling Section dispatched a commando team with orders to investigate and recover any werewolves they found.

The operation was not an unqualified success. In capturing the beast, three commandos were killed and two more were wounded. To complicate matters further, local landowner Sir John Talbot, on whose land the hunt took place, insisted on taking charge of the captured werewolf himself. Colonel John Bevan, the head of the London Controlling Section, was overruled when he tried to dismiss the landowner's demands. Talbot was a cousin of the earls of Shrewsbury, and during World War I he had served in the Imperial Camel Corps in Somaliland alongside Lord Ismay, now Military Deputy Secretary to the British Cabinet and a personal friend of Winston Churchill.

To Bevan's dismay, the matter of the Llanwelly werewolf was taken completely out of his hands: the suspected werewolf and the wounded commandos were never heard of again. In a letter preserved in the Imperial War Museum, Bevan speculates angrily that the werewolf was a close friend or relative of Talbot's, and he went over Bevan's head to protect the family name.

The truth of the matter seems to lie in the interagency rivalries that plagued Allied clandestine operations at this time. Having heard reports of Germany's embryonic *Werewolf* program, Churchill had decided to develop his own lycanthropic troops. The Talbot Group, as the operation was called, was housed on the family's estate outside Llanwelly, and although its existence is still officially denied its werewolf troops saw action in Norway, the Ardennes, and Bavaria.

A 12th-century wall painting of St. Cuthbert from Durham Cathedral. (Holmes Garden Photos / Alamy)

The position of the Talbot Group within the command structure of the British Army remains unclear. Its members are rumored to have acted in support of SAS operations in various parts of the world, and some Argentinian reports from the Falklands Conflict of 1982 suggest that British werewolves were seen on East Falkland in the days leading up to the British landings. The group's name also appears on UNPROFOR (United Nations Protection Force) flight manifests from the Bosnian conflict, and in confidential briefings from Iraq and Afghanistan. However, no details on the group's activities in those conflicts can be found.

It seems, though, that the Talbot Group has had some success in turning werewolves into soldiers. It is even rumored that some volunteers from the SAS, the Parachute Regiment, the Royal Marines, and other elite British units have volunteered to join the Talbot Group and become werewolves.

When in the field, the werewolves of the Talbot Group generally masquerade as British troops, often wearing the insignia of forward reconnaissance units, or as private military contractors. Their equipment is consistent with their cover: L85 rifles and L86A1 Light Support Weapons are the standard weapons and Land Rovers are the most common vehicles. The group's operations extend into almost every aspect of irregular and paranormal warfare, and they are known to have deployed "capture teams" into areas of suspected werewolf activity.

The Yokai Jingcha

The Japanese *Yokai Jingcha* ("supernatural constabulary") trace their origins back to 1603, when Shogun Tokugawa Ieyasu appointed Ogata Hideto to the newly created office of *yokai-bugyo* (roughly, "commissioner for supernatural creatures") as part of his overhaul of Japanese government. Ogata developed a network of contacts throughout Japan, mainly Shinto priests who served as needed. Local legends and incident reports were sent to Edo, where they were analyzed and compiled into the *Yokai Motocho*, a central register of Japan's supernatural population.

Over the following three centuries the office developed into a government department. In 1874 it was expanded and reorganized under its current name. Today, it has field offices in every prefecture of Japan, supported by research and logistics departments in Tokyo.

Because Japanese *hengeyokai* are rarely violent, the *Yokai Jingcha* consists primarily of seasoned investigators, making it different from the SWAT-style units of many other nations. The average age of new recruits is 37, much older than in Japan's other specialist police branches. Candidates are selected for a combination of exemplary police service and detailed local knowledge, and given additional training in the field of supernatural investigation. The Tokyo office is home to the *Yokai Kidotai* ("supernatural riot unit"), which can be airlifted to any location in Japan within two hours.

Investigators normally dress in business suits like detectives from other police services. They are not routinely armed, although tasers are becoming popular. The *Yokai Kidotai* carries standard riot police equipment, including 15 pounds of body armor, riot shields, and batons. Capture squads use forked "man catcher" poles in conjunction with shields, crowding a target into a confined space for darting or netting. Kill missions are authorized only in extreme circumstances.

The *Yokai Jincha* has no mandate to operate outside Japan, but senior investigators occasionally travel to attend conferences and act as advisors.

The Order of St. Cuthbert

The position of the Catholic Church has always been that werewolves do not exist, and that it is a sin even to believe in them. As early as the 8th century AD, St Boniface wrote that upon their baptism, converts to Christianity must renounce "trusting in witches and a superstitious fear of werewolves." Records of medieval werewolf trials in France and elsewhere invariably conclude that the accused was either acting under a delusion or had put on the form of a wolf through witchcraft.

This position has remained official policy to the present day. The 18th-century Benedictine monk Augustin Calmet makes only a passing mention of werewolves in his wide-ranging *Traité sur les Apparitions et sur les Vampires* ("Treatise on Ghosts and Vampires"), dismissing lycanthropy as a delusion brought about by witchcraft or suggestion. As late as 1933, Montague Summers continued to promulgate this view in his book *The Werewolf*.

Despite this, the Inquisition – first under its own name, and later as the Sacred Congregation of the Holy Office and the Congregation for the Doctrine of the Faith – has maintained a small but active sub-branch devoted to the investigation of lycanthropy, which is known today as the Order of St.

Cuthbert. It will be remembered that this early Northumbrian saint is a patron of shepherds, the wolf's natural enemy.

From documents available in the public domain, it seems that the Order was founded around 1760 in Sainte-Colombe-de-Peyre, a small village on the pilgrimage route of St. James of Compostela. It is interesting to note that just a few years later, the nearby Gévaudan district was plagued by a notorious beast which may or may not have been a werewolf.

The Order's present-day headquarters is thought to be at Ushaw College, a former Catholic seminary that is now a part of the University of Durham in northern England, which was founded in 1808 as St. Cuthbert's College – not to be confused with St. Cuthbert's Society, which was founded 80 years later as an Anglican college within Durham University.

The only surviving photograph of General Mikhail Zaroff.

Members of the Order have been active in many parts of the world, frequently operating under the cover of Catholic charities and aid organizations. In Bosnia, the Order worked with local Franciscans to track Serbian and other groups that made use of wolf imagery, and separate genuine werewolf packs from simple bandits and war criminals.

More recently, the Order sponsored an extensive study of the *chupacabra* in North and Central America. As a result several public reports were issued that concluded – neatly in line with Church policy – that the creature was no monster, but simply a coyote (or sometimes a raccoon) suffering from a particular kind of mange.

The Inquisition remains active worldwide, secretly investigating reports of lycanthropy and other paranormal phenomena. The Order of St. Cuthbert takes the lead in werewolf investigations, but the main body of the Inquisition provides logistical support and firepower as required. A typical investigative team will consist of one member of the Order and one or more specialists from other branches of the Inquisition, supported by a fire team from the Swiss Guard. Typical cover identities include Catholic aid or charity workers, missionaries, or anthropologists from a European or American university.

Equipment varies, and some can be locally acquired. Guns and other military equipment usually come from the armories of the Swiss Guard: Glock 9mm automatic pistols and Heckler & Koch MP7 and UMP submachine guns are standard. Ground vehicles are almost always sourced locally, and vary widely.

Like the rest of the Inquisition, the Order of St. Cuthbert maintains very few bases of its own. Normally it counts on other local Church organizations for accommodation and local knowledge. The Order is known to have strong ties with Franciscans around the world, and through the Inquisition it can also count on the support of Dominican assets. It is thought to be less close to the Jesuits, who are rumored to have a small force of monster-hunters attached to their exorcist arm.

The Zaroff Society

Mikhail Zaroff (1882–1924) was a Don Cossack who had risen to the rank of general by the time of the Russian Revolution. His twin passions were war and hunting, and after the fall of the Russian Empire he traveled the world seeking out the most dangerous game. With the wealth he had smuggled out of Russia he was able to purchase a small island in a remote corner of the Caribbean, and set about turning its jungle terrain into a private hunting park.

Various unsavory rumors were circulated about Zaroff in the years following his death, apparently in a hunting accident. According to certain American newspapers, he had become bored with big game, and took to hunting shipwreck victims in his search for a more challenging quarry. Despite decades of claim and counter-claim, these charges have never been substantiated.

What is known for sure is that Zaroff sought out the company of the world's greatest hunters, and seldom refused an invitation to join a safari or an expedition into unknown territory. He accompanied Colonel Percy Fawcett into the jungles of Brazil, and traveled to Tibet in search of the yeti. The archives of the Royal Geographical Society have a letter from Zaroff accepting a place as a tracker on N. A. Tombazi's 1925 expedition to Tibet, but Zaroff died before the expedition set out.

The Zaroff Society claims to be descended from the general's coterie of fellow hunters, and its stated purpose is to seek out the most dangerous game in the world. Among its trophies are several large pelts claimed to have come from werewolves, as well as South American were-jaguars and African were-hyenas. The Society's library is said to contain first-hand accounts of werewolves and their behavior written by members – as well as an angry letter from Ernest Hemingway, protesting the rejection of his application for membership.

The Society has discreet houses in many of the world's great cities, and in gateway cities such as Mombasa, Cape Town, Lagos, Rio de Janeiro, Bucharest, and Lhasa. Its expeditions often pose as private safaris, but have also moved under the guise of archaeological, zoological, or geological expeditions: the Society maintains ties with some of the most prestigious universities in Europe and North America for this specific purpose. Since about 1980, the Society has increasingly used oil exploration as a cover story: it has members at the highest levels of Middle Eastern politics and royalty, whose influence can open doors in parts of the world where Western universities cannot.

The equipment of a Society expedition is always the newest and the best. Thanks to the enormous wealth of many Society members, cost is never an issue. High-powered rifles with telescopic sights are the standard hunting weapon, but are backed up by machine pistols and large-caliber handguns for personal defense; equipment is almost always the property of individual members, and not of the Society. Some Society members also take great pride in their mastery of archaic and exotic hunting weapons, deeming a kill made with a primitive weapon more valuable than one made with high-tech modern equipment.

Glossary

BIGFOOT A mythic, large, hairy creature purportedly seen in northwestern America.

CANDIDATE A person or thing likely to receive a particular fate.

DELUSION An impression that is believed despite being contradicted by what is generally accepted as reality.

DEMONIC Characteristic of demons or evil spirits.

GRIEVOUS Describing something very severe or serious.

HALLUCINATION A perception of something not present.

HYPNOSIS The state of consciousness in which a person apparently loses the power of voluntary action.

INFESTATION Invaded or overrun by organisms or beings.

LYCANTHROPE Werewolf.

MANIFESTATION A display or demonstration by an act or appearance.

MELANCHOLY A feeling of sadness, usually with no obvious cause.

METAMORPHOSIS To change from one form to another.

NOTORIOUS Famous for some bad quality.

OCCULT Supernatural, mystical, or magical beliefs, practices, or phenomena.

PAGAN A person who has religious beliefs other than those of the main world.

PARANORMAL Phenomena that are beyond the scope of normal scientific understanding.

PHENOMENON A fact or situation that exists or has happened.

POSSESSED Controlled by an evil spirit.

PREDATOR Something that ruthlessly exploits others.

SUBSTANTIATE To provide evidence to support or prove the truth of.

For More Information

American Society for Psychical Research, Inc. (ASPR)
5 West 73rd Street
New York, NY 10023
(212) 799-5050
Website: http://www.aspr.com
This organization's mission is to explore extraordinary or unexplained phenomena that have been called psychic or paranormal and their implications for our understanding of consciousness, the universe, and the nature of existence. It addresses questions with scientific research and offers educational activities, including lectures and conferences.

Parapsychological Association, Inc. (PA)
PO Box 24173
Columbus, OH 43224
(202) 318-2364
Website: http://www.parapsych.org
The Parapsychological Association is the international professional organization of scientists and scholars engaged in the study of "psi" (or "psychic") experiences, such as telepathy, clairvoyance, and psychic healing. The PA endorses no ideologies or beliefs other than the value of rigorous scientific and scholarly inquiry.

TAPS *ParaMagazine*
P.O. Box 233
Fly Creek, NY 13337
Email: jvj@tapsparamag.com
Website: www.tapsparamag.com
Founded by the Atlantic Paranormal Society (TAPS) in 2008, *ParaMagazine* is America's premiere paranormal print and digital publication, featuring the top minds on the topics of paranormal investigations, cryptozoology, ufology, and spiritual beliefs.

WEBSITES

Because of the changing nature of internet links, Rosen Publishing has developed an online list of websites related to the subject of this book. This site is updated regularly. Please use this link to access the list:

http://www.rosenlinks.com/MH/werewolves

For Further Reading

Buckland, Raymond. *The Weiser Field Guide to Ghosts: Apparitions, Spirits, Spectral Lights, and Other Hauntings of History and Legend.* San Francisco, CA: Weiser Books, 2009.

Curran, Bob. *Encyclopedia of the Undead: A Field Guide to Creatures That Cannot Rest in Peace.* Franklin Lakes, NJ: New Page Books, 2006.

Curran, Bob. *Werewolves: A Field Guide to Shapeshifters, Lycanthropes, and Man-Beasts.* Franklin Lakes, NJ: New Page Books, 2009.

Duncan, Ritch, and Bob Powers. *The Werewolf's Guide to Life: A Manual for the Newly Bitten.* New York, NY: Broadway Books, 2009.

Guiley, Rosemary. *The Encyclopedia of Vampires & Werewolves.* New York, NY: Facts on File, 2011.

Konstantinos. *Werewolves: The Occult Truth.* Woodbury, MN: Llewellyn Publications, 2010.

Krulos, Tea. *Monster Hunters: On the Trail with Ghost Hunters, Bigfooters, Ufologists, and Other Paranormal Investigators.* Chicago, IL: Chicago Review, 2015.

Mogk, Matt. *Everything You Ever Wanted to Know About Zombies.* New York, NY: Gallery Books, 2011.

Peck, M. Scott. *Glimpses of the Devil: A Psychiatrist's Personal Accounts of Possession, Exorcism, and Redemption.* New York, NY: Free Press, 2009.

Schwalb, Suzanne, and Margaret Rubiano. *Vampires, Werewolves, Zombies: Compendium Monstrum: From the Papers of Herr Doktor Max Sturm & Baron Ludwig Von Drang.* White Plains, NY: Peter Pauper Press, 2010.

Steiger, Brad. *The Werewolf Book: The Encyclopedia of Shape-Shifting Beings.* Canton, MI: Visible Ink Press, 2012.

Sugg, Richard. *Mummies, Cannibals, and Vampires: The History of Corpse Medicine from the Renaissance to the Victorians.* New York, NY: Routledge, 2011.

Wasik, Bill, and Monica Murphy. *Rabid: A Cultural History of the World's Most Diabolical Virus.* New York, NY: Penguin Books, 2013.

Index